The Yellow Rose

A volume in
The Hispanic Population in the United States
Richard R. Verdugo, *Series Editor*

The Yellow Rose

Racial Stratification in a Mexican American Community

Richard R. Verdugo

IAP

INFORMATION AGE PUBLISHING, INC.
Charlotte, NC • www.infoagepub.com

Library of Congress Cataloging-in-Publication Data

A CIP record for this book is available from the Library of Congress
http://www.loc.gov

ISBN: 978-1-64113-641-9 (Paperback)
978-1-64113-642-6 (Hardcover)
978-1-64113-643-3 (ebook)

Printed and bound by CPI Group (UK) Ltd, Croydon, CR0 4YY

Contents

Preface

In the early spring of 1969, a letter arrived in the office of William "Bill" V. D'Antonio, chair and professor of sociology, University of Notre Dame. The letter was from Jesse Daffron, a former student of the university. Daffron wanted to know if Professor D'Antonio would be interested in conducting a comprehensive social survey of his community, Fabens, Texas.

As a life-long resident of Fabens, Daffron was extremely concerned with the towns' slow, and persistent economic decline. He had come to the conclusion that a study of the community was needed prior to developing plans that would hopefully steer the community into a more prosperous path. By chance, Professor D'Antonio was scheduled to deliver a lecture in El Paso in mid-April and arranged to meet with Daffron where they could talk at length about a possible research study of the community. D'Antonio had recently published a book on influentials in two border cities with William Form, and was very interested in conducting such a study.

From his meeting with Daffron, D'Antonio concluded that a study was "feasible, worthwhile, and could, in fact, be of great mutual benefit." As a result of this somewhat modest meeting, one of only a handful of Chicano community studies in the United States originated.

The study of the Fabens community was conducted in the summer of 1969 by a University of Notre Dame research team headed by Professors D'Antonio (sociology) and Irwin Press (anthropology). D'Antonio is currently an IPR Fellow, Institute for Policy Research and Catholic Studies, Catholic University of American in Washington, DC. Irwin Press is currently

The Yellow Rose, pages ix–xvii

emeritus professor in the Department of Anthropology, University of Notre Dame. Other members of the research team were three young students: Timothy Johnson (deceased), Saskia Sassen (currently professor of sociology, Columbia University), and Gary Gereffi (currently professor of sociology, Duke University).

A report was completed in early 1970, and though a book publication was planned, other commitments stalled these plans indefinitely. The report and several large boxes of materials from the project were stored in Professor Press' attic.

In late Spring of 1985, nearly 17 years later from the time Daffron's letter had arrived in D'Antonio's office, D'Antonio and I were having lunch near the offices of the American Sociological Association in Washington, DC. D'Antonio and I had been on friendly terms for several years. The conversation, as it frequently did, turned to sociological research. As our conversation proceeded, D'Antonio remembered the Fabens study. He had completely forgotten about it, and wasn't quite sure what had become of the report and all the materials. He would do some checking and asked if I would like to look at the report; perhaps I could do something with it. I was stunned. Of course I would look at it.

Within several weeks Bill called my office to inform me that he had contacted Irwin Press and the report had recently arrived in his office at the American Sociological Association (ASA) headquarters. He asked if I would like to come over to the ASA offices and pick up the manuscript. I was there within an hour. After spending several weeks studying the original manuscript, it became clear that I needed the other documents if I was ever to gain a firm grasp of the project. I called Bill and asked if other materials existed and could I have access to them. He would check with Irwin Press.

About a month later, Bill called my office with the news that additional materials had arrived. There was a problem, however. The materials were contained in three very large boxes. I took a cab over to the ASA offices, carried the boxes into the cab and managed to get them up to my office. I would later haul them to my home.

I spent the next 3 years, off and on, re-reading the manuscript and pouring over all the materials. The materials themselves consist of field notes, newspaper clippings, numerous letters, notes and outlines for the report, and various abstracts of pertinent literature. I was slowly becoming familiar with the project—its purpose and the hardships endured by the study team in conducting their research.

I then began my own outlines for re-doing the manuscript with the hope of publishing a book. In addition, I also wrote several short background papers in an effort to flesh out theoretical problems and to acquire additional knowledge about Texas history. It wasn't until the summer of 1990 that the book's main objective began to crystalize. There were two questions I felt would drive the study:

1. Why is this study important (especially since it is such an old data set)?
2. What theoretical framework could best organizethe study?

There are four basic reasons why this is an important study. First, it is one of only a few studies of a predominantly Chicano community ever conducted. It would thus add greatly to that genre of social science research concerned with the history of Chicanos in the United States. Indeed, Albert Camarillo (1979) has this to say about Chicano history:

> As scholars discern the major patterns of the Chicano experience, the history of Mexican people in the United States, which has been be-clouded by misinterpretation and neglect, will be more fully understood. (p. 2)

Second, the study was conducted in 1969, a time in America's history before the Chicano movement significantly affected the socio-political climate throughout the Southwest. It also lays the groundwork for a possible follow-up of the Fabens community.

Third, data from the study would greatly enhance our understanding of stratification systems: how they evolve and how they affect other institutions, not only in general, but in rural societies. Indeed, the richness of the data would inform social scientists about how social structures emerge.

Fourth, it is, in essence, an addition to the evolution and development of American society. From a small Mexican village, to Anglo arrival and control, it is a microscopic view of a general pattern that occurred throughout Texas and the American Southwest.

A theoretical framework was needed. Such a theoretical framework that could best describe the study would have at least three major components: the meeting of two distinct cultures where one has greater power than the other; the emergence of a race-based social structure over time; and that such a system permeates all aspects of society. I develop a theoretical framework in the following section.

Framework

The term "theoretical framework" sounds rather formidable, and, indeed, the manner in which some theories are presented leads many to formulate a negative image of theory. Theory, however, is not intended to make research complex, but, rather, to provide a lucid picture of a complex research problems. From the Fabens study, I have a mountain of historical information on the community that needs—indeed, begs for—organization. That is, a viewpoint or framework that makes sense of the major historical events that have taken place in the Fabens community. Theory should be parsimonious.

Racial stratification is an appropriate framework describing a system of structured inequality, where access to scarce and desired resources is based on ethnic/racial group membership. Racial stratification assigns roles and functions to individuals based on their ethnic-racial group membership. These assignments have both physical and social consciousness consequences.

Though stratification systems vary across time and space, two of its primary components appear to be ubiquitous: *ideological* and *structural*. Stratification systems have *ideologies* justifying their existence and have ranged from "the will of God" to those alleging biological superiority. Bierstedt (1963) noted that "an ideology is an idea supported by a norm" (p. 171). Ideologies, then, encompass norms, mores, folkways, values, and theories. Ideologies provide explanations for the order of things and, more importantly, they are rooted in group interests (Mannheim 1936, Ch. 2).[1]

Structural mechanisms are a second component of stratification systems. Structural mechanisms involve the regular and patterned forms of separate or unequal treatment of groups. There are two such components: *behavioral* and *physical*. Examples of behavioral mechanisms include the norms and values that lead to inequitable treatment and discrimination—these normative concepts become institutionaized in the social system. Housing and occupational segregation are examples of the physical mechanisms characterizing stratification systems. Structural mechanisms, then, involve specific kinds of social interactions, including the separation of groups. Segregation an group isolation are examples of the physical aspects of racial stratification.

Structural and ideological mechanisms not only reinforce one another, but they also serve to justify and maintain a specific kind of social order. There is a built-in tautology to their relationship: an ideology justifies differential treatment or structural separation, and a given structure, in turn, perpetuates and reinforces an ideology (e.g., group norms, values, and stereotypes).

A system of racial stratification exists if race and ethnic group membership are the basis for a system of structured inequality.[2] Race and ethnicity are used as a "way of classifying people and their functions, of prescribing which sorts of people should do what sort of things" (Hodges 1964, p. 8). The overall effect of racial stratification is the separation of racial groups, both physically and in the social conscience (see Blank, Dabady, & Citra, 2004; see also Ossowski 1966).

The historical events that have transformed Fabens into a system of race-based inequality are nicely captured by a racial stratification framework. By stratification is meant differentiation; and thus racial stratification means differentiation based on racial group membership. In such a system, ethnic-racial minorities most often, though not completely, occupy the lower rungs of the socioeconomic ladder. Moreover, and this is exceedingly significant, racial stratification permeates all aspects of society; that is, it penetrates all of society's major social institutions. How such a system comes to exist, however, is an entirely different question, and forms the second part of my framework.

When two distinct cultures meet it does not necessarily follow that a racial stratification system emerges. The absolutely crucial factor that must be present for a racial stratification system to emerge is an imbalance of power between groups. Under these circumstances one group can impose its will despite the objections of the other. But how long can one group continue to impose its will on another simply by resorting to its power advantage? It clearly cannot go on indefinitely because it becomes impractical. It is here that a third, and final, component of my framework comes into play–the ideological.

Marx made the following observation: The ruling ideas in society are the ideas of the ruling class. A normative system of ideas, views, folkways, mores, and so on, is developed by those in power and used to define the roles and the expected individual/group behaviors in a social system. These norms and ideas become institutionalized in the culture and infiltrate all major social institutions, such as the educational system, the economy, and politics. In short, an institutionalized ideological system upholds a system of racial stratification.

Given my racial stratification framework, how, then, did racial stratification emerge in Fabens? The answer to this question is that it did not differ from what generally occurred throughout the state of Texas. The political scientist, Mario Barrera (1981) has suggested that three historical events worked to shape racial stratification in Texas: the Mexican–American War, displacement of the indigenous population from their land, and the emergence of a segmented labor force.

The Mexican–American War had important effects on race relations not only in Fabens but throughout Texas. To begin with, the war heightened the already intense relations between Mexicans and Anglos. Second, it led to the eventual annexation of what now comprises all of the Southwestern portions of the United States.

The displacement of the indigenous population from their land was a second factor and was related in an important way to the Mexican–American War. When the Southwest was annexed to the United States, the indigenous population, who had previously been under rule of the Mexican government, were given the choice to move into Mexican territory, or stay in what was now U.S. territory. Those who chose to remain in the United States found themselves under U.S. jurisdiction and all that it entailed. And, as it turned out, it was more than they had bargained for. The indigenous population now faced two structural aspects that would forever change the complexion of their lives: taxes on their land, and, in addition, the burden of showing proof of land ownership. These policies were unheard of during Mexican rule.

Finally, there was the emergence of a segmented labor force, where nearly the entire indigenous population either occupied the worst jobs or were unemployed and formed a large cadre of cheap surplus labor, at the beckoning of manipulative employers.

Data from the 1850 Census may be used in estimating the size of the Mexican population residing at that point in American history. Data are displayed by states as they existed at that time (see Table P.1).

Two years after the treaty with Mexico was signed, ending the Mexican–American War, approximately 84,550 Mexicans decided to stay in what was now the United States of America. There are several interesting pieces of information regarding this group of Mexicans—the first Mexican Americans. To begin with, the larger percentage were males. Indeed, 56% of the Mexican American population were men. The discrepancy may be due to the harsh life in the frontier. This would also be the case among non-Hispanic settlers in years to come as the American population moved west.

Secondly, Mexican Americans were a young population. Forty percent were Age 19 and younger. As one moves from youth to middle age to old age, the percentages significantly decline (see Figure P.1).

Third, the vast majority of Mexican Americans lived in the West. Indeed, nearly 90% resided in the West. Also, the vast majority of Mexican Americans resided in rural areas and it was impossible to identify cities in which they might have resided.

The status of Mexican Americans in the United States was not positive. Three factors were inextricably related and lay the groundwork for making Mexican Americans second class citizens: land, war, and labor. Land

TABLE P.1 Selected Demographic Traits of Mexican Americans: 1850

	Frequency	Percentage
Gender		
Male	47,009	55.599
Female	37,541	44.401
Total	84,550	100.000
Age		
0 to 9	21,212	25.088
10 to 19	19,223	22.735
20 to 29	17,498	20.695
30 to 39	10,768	12.735
40 to 49	7,857	9.293
50 to 59	4,273	5.054
60 to 69	2,419	2.860
70 to 79	507	0.599
80+	794	0.939
Total	84,550	100.000
Region		
NE	283	0.334
MW	198	0.234
SO	9,076	10.734
WE	74,994	88.698
Total	84,550	100.000
Urbanization		
Urban	6,206.80	7.341
Rural	78,343.00	92.659
Total	84,549.80	100.000

Source: Ruggles, Genadek, Goeken, Grover, & Sobek (2015)

displacement could not have occurred without the annexation, which could not have occurred without the Mexican–American War, and the emergence of a segmented labor force was given a boost by the displacement of the Mexican population from their land. All three factors, then, colluded in creating a large army of displaced persons, driven from their land to seek jobs at a time when the United States was pushing westward, driven by the ideology of "manifest destiny." I cannot overemphasize the economic boom this was for the United States, for example, the vast natural resources and cheap labor with which to exploit these resources.

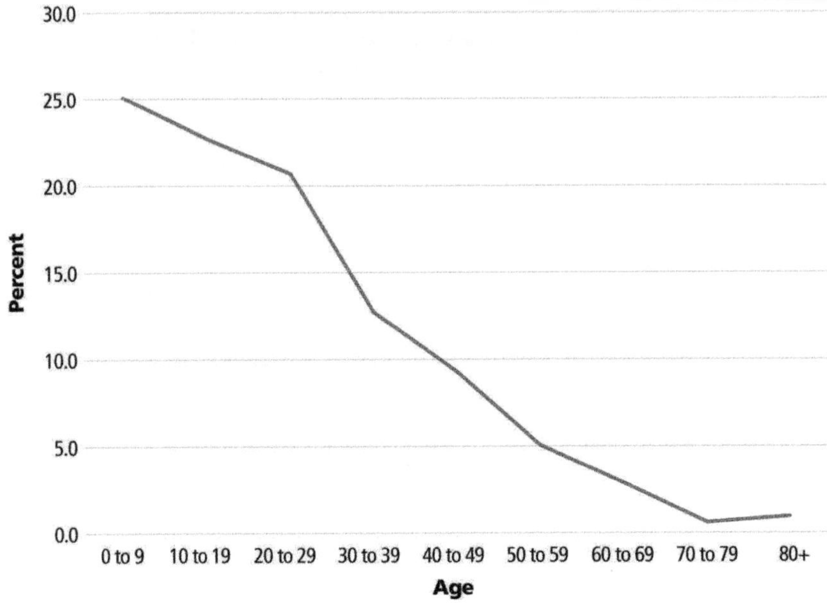

Figure P.1 Percentages by age intervals among Mexican Americans: 1850. *Source:* Ruggles, Genadek, Goeken, Grover & Sobek (2017).

In the chapters to follow, I present and discuss historical examples of each factor as well as their significance in the evolution of Fabens, Texas as a racially stratified community. As such, the book is composed of two parts. Part one, the early years, describes Fabens before Anglo arrival and then during the period when Anglos began to arrive. Anglos arriving in the area resulted in a clash of cultures and to frequent violent confrontations.

Part two is devoted to examining the results from the 1969 community survey conducted by the Notre Dame Research team, and comprises the bulk of my study. The main focus in part two is in examining several social institutions, such as the educational system and the polity. These investigations are intended to point out how racial stratification infiltrated each institution and the effect it has had on the community. In essence, the economic decline of the community, as was the case in 1969, I would argue, is directly related to the racial stratification system characterizing Fabens—a system too rigid to be of any use and which only inhibits economic progress.

Notes

1. The most obvious ideological view held by dominant group members is racism. Racism as used in this chapter is similar to that of Wilson's (1973, pp. 32–33). Wilson states that there are two components of racism: biological and cultural. While biological racism preaches inherent inferiority of subordinate groups, cultural racism maintains that subordinate groups are culturally inferior, and with the proper training can better themselves. Also, see Ogbu (1978, pp. 131–147) for a discussion of the subtle mechanisms of racial stratification.
2. Racial stratification is not unlike other forms of group differentiation. For a definition of social stratification see Lenski (1966). For other definitions of racial stratification see Blalock (1967), Lieberson (1961), and Olsen (1970). Moreover, there is some agreement among scholars that racial stratification systems arise when the following conditions are present: (a) contact between two or more races, (b) one group has a power advantage, (c) there is competition over scarce and desired resources, and (d) ethnocentrism/racism exists (Noel, 1968; Wilson 1973). For an excellent discussion see H. Edward Ransford (1977, especially Chapters 2 and 3).

1

The Demography of the Mexican-American Population, 1960 to 1970

Texas and the United States

Diversity is a major factor in the experiences and demographic profiles of Mexican Americans. For example, their experiences in Texas are based on severe conflict and violence. In New Mexico, Mexican Americans were a larger share of the population and there was also a group of elites that moved into important political offices and made their experiences less dependent on conflict. (Moore & Cuellar, 1970). Differences in the experiences may also be highlighted by differences in demographic traits. In this chapter I briefly describe the demographic profile of Mexican Americans in 1960 and 1970.

Under the Treaty of Guadalupe Hidalgo of 1848, the United States acquired the lands that eventually became California, Texas, New Mexico, Arizona, Colorado, and Nevada.

The Yellow Rose, pages 1–6

Size of the Mexican American Population

Between the years of 1960–1970, the Mexican-American community grew at a faster rate, nationally, than did the Mexican community in Texas. In 1960, the national Mexican-American population stood at 4.02 million persons. By 1970 it had increased to 5.4 million persons, or an increase of 34.9% over the 1960 to 1970 period. In Texas, the increase was from 1.5 million in 1960 to 1.8 million by 1970, or an increase of 15.5%.

Composition of the Mexican American Population: Nationally and in Texas

Table 1.1 presents selected socio-demographic data on the Mexican-American population in the United States in 1970.

Age

Mexican Americans, as a population, were younger than non-Mexican Americans. In 1960, the mean age among non-Hispanics was 31.3, and 23.2 among Mexican Americans. By 1970 there was a slight increase: non-Hispanics, 32.1, and Mexican Americans, 24.2.

There was a slight difference in the sex distribution between non-Hispanics and Mexican Americans, particularly in 1970. In 1960, sex differences between the two ethnic groups were minor, but in 1970 non-Hispanic females had a 3% advantage over non-Hispanic males. In contrast, the sex differences among Mexican Americans continued to be minor. The difference may be due to the older age among non-Hispanics, and the life expectancy among women is greater than that of men.

One way of testing my conjecture is by computing sex ratios for both non-Hispanics and Mexican Americans for both 1960 and 1970. These data are displayed in Figure 1.1. Note that at older ages, the ratios both in 1960 and in 1970 favor Mexican Americans. In short, among non-Hispanics, women are considerably more likely to outlive men; while among Mexican Americans women outlive men, though the difference is not as drastic as in the non-Hispanic population.

Education

Non-Hispanics attained more education than Mexican Americans, in both 1960 and in 1970. In 1960, 59% of non-Hispanics age 25+ had not

TABLE 1.1 Demographic Traits of Mexican Americans Compared to Non Hispanics, 1960 and 1970

	Frequencies and Means				Percents (Where Applicable)			
	1960		1970		1960		1970	
	NH	MA	NH	MA	NH	MA	NH	MA
Population Size	173,499,552	4,024,313	194,029,900	5,428,900				
Age								
Means	31.3	23.2	32.1	24.2				
Sex								
Male	85,257,640	2,019,520	94,107,100	2,684,100	49.1%	50.6%	48.5%	49.4%
Female	88,316,240	1,974,320	99,922,800	2,744,800	50.9%	49.4%	51.5%	50.6%
Education								
< High School	56,558,300	1,316,860	49,588,000	1,536,700	58.5%	80.7%	46.9%	70.3%
High School	23,033,460	197,380	33,286,800	433,400	23.8%	12.1%	31.5%	19.8%
Some College	9,614,780	77,180	11,357,900	135,100	9.9%	4.7%	10.8%	6.2%
College+	7,524,480	40,120	11,396,600	79,800	7.8%	2.5%	10.8%	3.7%
Jobs								
Professional	11,876,560	94,780	16,701,900	181,900	18.6%	7.8%	22.9%	11.0%
Service	5,984,120	124,880	7,593,600	202,500	9.3%	10.2%	10.4%	12.2%
Clerical	8,628,360	95,940	11,232,100	183,700	13.5%	7.9%	15.4%	11.1%
Sales	4,987,100	59,820	6,197,000	99,100	7.8%	4.9%	8.5%	6.0%
Craft	15,988,080	333,960	17,500,800	485,000	25.0%	27.4%	24.0%	29.3%
Operatives	4,844,300	109,400	7,617,400	268,800	7.6%	9.0%	10.4%	16.2%
House Service	600,900	13,220	700,200	25,300	0.9%	1.1%	1.0%	1.5%
Farm	3,733,860	176,440	2,432,900	134,600	5.8%	14.5%	3.3%	8.1%
Military	1,699,300	26,360	1,963,800	32,900	2.7%	2.2%	2.7%	2.0%
Labor	2,469,340	113,140	986,200	41,500	3.9%	9.3%	1.4%	2.5%
Unknown	3,205,140	70,700	2,000	0	5.0%	5.8%	0.0%	0.0%
Wages								
Means	4,031	2,975	5,881	4,541				

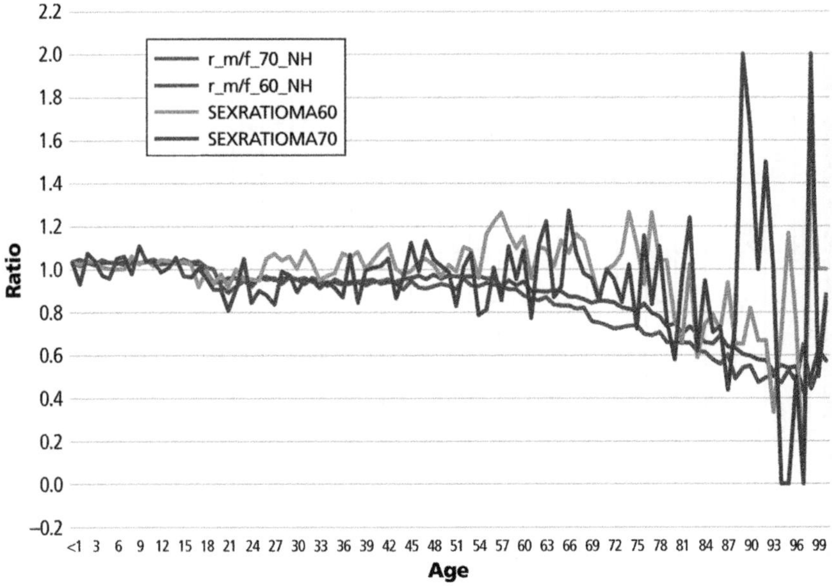

Figure 1.1 Sex ratios among non-Hispanics and Mexican Americans by age, 1960 and 1970. *Source*: Ruggles et al. (2017)

completed high school. The figure for Mexican Americans was 81%. By 1970, the percentages were 47% and 70%, respectively.

High school graduation is also an important educational marker. In 1960, 24% of non-Hispanics had graduated from high school as their terminal degree, and only 12% among Mexican Americans. In 1970, the percentages were 32% among non-Hispanics and 20% among Mexican Americans.

Finally, in the 20th and 21st centuries, a college education has replaced a high school diploma to enhance the chances of one's economic status. In 1960, 8% of non-Hispanics had completed college, and only 2.5% of Mexican Americans had achieved such an educational status. In 1970, the college disadvantage experienced by Mexican Americans continued. Eleven percent of non-Hispanics had completed college, while only 4% of Mexican Americans had completed college.

Wages

Non-Hispanic workers age 16–64 have wages greater than Mexican American workers of the same age. Moreover, it appears that the wage gap increased over the 1960–1970 period.

In 1960, the average wage for non-Hispanic workers was $4,033, and $2,976 for Mexican American workers. By 1970, the average wages for non-Hispanic and Mexican American workers were $5,881 and $4,541, respectively. Note that the wage gap increased from $1,157 in 1960 to $1,340 by 1970.

Job Status

There are significant differences in job placement between non-Hispanics and Mexican American workers. Data are displayed in Figure 1.2. Of the 11 occupational titles listed, including military status and an unknown occupation, the biggest occupational gaps are among professional jobs, clericals, employment in a farm related job, and general labor jobs.

I also computed indices of dissimilarity for 1960 and 1970. The index tells us how much of a percentage change has to occur in order for two distributions to be equal. My calculations indicate there was little change in occupational equality over the 10 year period, 1960 to 1970. In 1960, the dissimilarity was .395, and .390 by 1970.

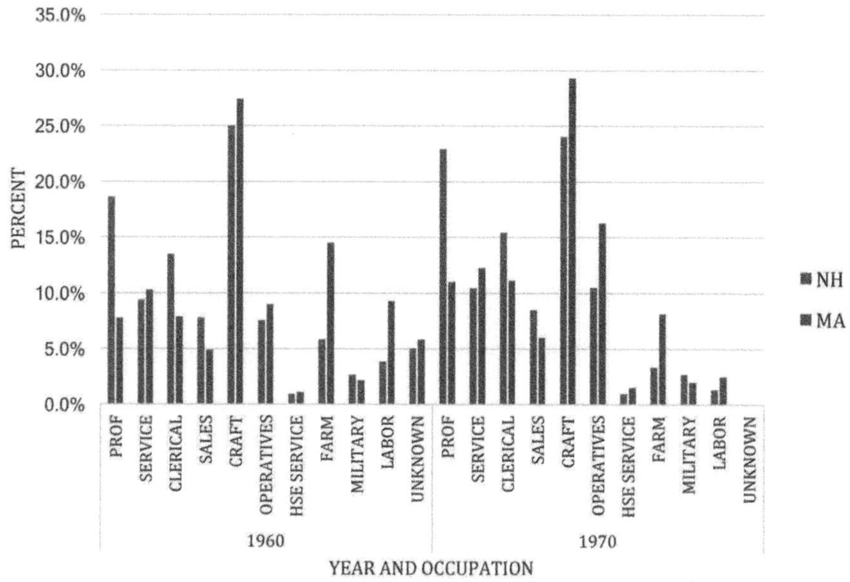

Figure 1.2 Occupational distribution among non-Hispanics and Mexican American workers, Age 16+, 1960 and 1970.

Four occupations displayed the greatest difference, in both 1960 and 1970. In other words, these four occupations appear to drive occupational differentiation between non-Hispanic and Mexican American workers. These occupations are professional, clerical, farm-related jobs, and labor.

2

Fabens in Years Prior to Anglo Arrival

There is speculation that there were inhabitants in Fabens before 1870, occupying a stagecoach stop at San Felipe in the sand dunes about 3 miles northeast of Fabens. However, the earliest sites on which there is reliable data are the settlements of La Isla, Cuadrilla, and Aldama, which were probably settled—in that order—in the late 1870s.

At that time there was a branch of the Rio Grande, which was then referred to as the Rio Bravo—a name citing its occasional great floods. Rio Bravo flowed along the route of the canal, which, in 1969, formed the southwest boundary of Fabens. It thus cut off a large portion of land called *La Isla* (the Island), before it joined the other branch further downstream. The oldest settlement in the area was near a grove of trees across the canal from Fabens, on the La Isla road.

Jesus Arroya was among the earliest settlers. Arroya owned 48 acres of land, including a small farm with approximately 50 cows. When he died in 1910, his sons, Abel and Federico, continued to work the farm.

The Yellow Rose, pages 7–10

Most of the early settlers of the Fabens area appear to have originated from San Elizario and included Juan Cordero who arrived in 1878, and Andres Telles. Other early settlers in Fabens (settling in La Isla) were Severo Cordero, Sabino Sierra, Nicolas Sierra, Bravorio Chavez, Sixto Salcido, Santiago Trujillo, and settlers with the last names Medina, Valenzuela, Escajeda, Holguin, and Vasquez.

The town of Cuadrilla, which is about 3 miles northwest of Fabens, and north of La Isla, took its name from the original four houses forming the corners of a square. Cuadrilla's early settlers included the families of Librado Beltran, Juan Alvarez, Erminio Ruiz, Gavino Loya, and the Madrid and Fierro families.

Aldama was located about a mile southeast of Fabens, and its early families included those of Esteban Perez, Jesus Bustillos, and Acosta. It consisted of about half a dozen houses and a chapel. In 1911, unfortunately, the entire town was washed away in a flood.

All three communities (La Isla, Cuadrilla, and Aldama) were essentially independent and self-contained. The communities have changed little from the time they were first settled and the time of the Mexican Revolution, about 1910. Changes that did occur included the arrival of a few families from San Elizario. Yet another change was the accumulation of resources by some Fabens families. For example, Juan Cordero owned 48 acres, but his initial holdings amounted to approximately 10 acres, and a small number goats and other draft animals. By the beginning of the 20th century, Cordero's stock increased to over 100 goats and six draft animals.

Cutting and hauling firewood was an occupation among early Fabens settlers. Once a week, someone from La Isla would take a train to El Paso with a large load of wood. Juan Cordero, in contrast, would often make the trip by mules. The money earned from the sale of firewood was used to purchase staples, such as cloth, which village women used in making clothes.

Families in the three communities grew their own food: corn, beans, gourds, watermelons, wheat, chiles, and vegetables. Families also kept goats and milk cows; fishing along the river banks was another source of food. Farms were small, mostly in the 48 acres or less range, and were individually owned.

La Isla had a stronger sense of community. The self-contained characteristic of farms was slightly different in La Isla. For example, during peak work periods all the men worked the land in common, moving from one farm to the next with no exchange in payment. The important periods of this common work activity were during the May planting, the June wheat harvest, the August corn harvest, and the September bean harvest. One interviewee noted that group activities were not conducted in Aldama or Cuadrilla, and suggested that its practice in other areas was due to the flooding that most often occurred in La Isla. The practice of helping one another also took place after extensive flood damage and rebuilding became necessary. The Rio Bravo wiped out the entire La Isla community in 1895 or 1896, and again in 1899 or 1900. During those periods, the Mexican government provided assistance to families in La Isla by permitting them to live, temporarily, in Juarez on small farms in El Colorado and San Augustine, southwest of the river.

There was no post office, school, doctor, or government office in the La Isla–Aldama–Cuadrilla area. However, the wife of Bravorio Chavez in La Isla served as a *curandera* (curer) in exchange for beans, corn, or grain, dispensing herbs and aiding in childbirths. Older males, including Juan Cordero and Sabino Sierra, acted as *dieron consejos* (providers of counsel) on simple questions of government; their counsel was mostly limited to reprimanding mischievous boys. Appeals or other forms of legal matters were rarely taken to the court in nearby San Elizario.

There was a chapel two miles west of what is now Fabens. The chapel was near the farms of Sabino Sierra, Bravorio Chavez, and Juan and Severo Cordero. The chapel was still standing in 1969.

The lifestyle, means of subsistence, and social organization among the three small villages were remarkably similar to those in the Mesilla Valley, just upriver from El Paso, prior to Anglo arrival in the 1870s. Both areas, in turn, seem to have shared a lifestyle and culture similar to that characterizing the early villages of 18th century New Mexico:

> Self-reliance was pervasive. Residents in the area produced most of their own foodstuff, built their own houses from local materials, manufactured furniture and other household items, and fashioned much of their own clothes and body ornaments. Most of the farms were small enough to be cultivated by a family.
>
> Patriarchy was the cultural norm in the Fabens area. Land was passed down from one generation to the next, and sub-divided if there was more than one son in a family. Sons remained with the family, together with their wives and children, until their father's death, at which time land would be divided among the sons. As settlements gradually increased in size and land available in the original grant was subdivided through inheritance, small groups left their parent's villages and started new settlements.
>
> Settlers built houses, maintained irrigation ditches, grazed their livestock, cared for their sick, buried their dead, and celebrated Catholic holy days. Neglected by both church and state, each village developed a relatively autonomous system of maintaining law and order, socializing children, and

> perpetuating their faith and culture. For men and boys, there might be an occasional excursion to a nearby city.
>
> Although livestock was brought into New Mexico by the very earliest Spanish settlers, the primary emphasis was farming of wheat, maize, beans, chili, other vegetables, and fruits. (González, 1967, pp. 38–43)
>
> Social organization/stratification mirrored that found in Mexico. Folklore and song, baptism, wedding and funeral customs, the compadrazgo–inheritance rules, beliefs, concerning health and disease, witchcraft, extended families living in multi-family dwellings, male authoritarianism, and many other factors in the Fabens area were either identical or very similar to those found in Mexico. Also, as in Mexico, those at the top of the class hierarchy were not only those who enjoyed greater wealth (based on land and or livestock, or both), but they also tended to be of purer Caucasian descent. These elites also were better educated; and many were either from a military family, or were descended from military leaders. The lowest class was composed of Indian slaves and servants, poor mestizos, and rural peasants, regardless of race. (González, 1967, pp. 29–30)

What differences existed may largely be attributed to the historical circumstances of armed conflict with Texans, and the instability and insecurity that characterizes young settlements. Also contributing to differences was the absence of upper-class patrones, at least on the U.S. side of the border. This class of Mexicans were absorbed by new American elites, which, by 1880, exerted control over the older settlements like San Elizario.

Therefore, prior to Anglo arrival, the Fabens area was rural, dotted by small farms with a considerable amount of self-reliance and community among its inhabitants. There was also a mild form of stratification based on wealth and race.

3

Anglo Arrival

The Mexican–American War, Land Displacement, and the Emergence of a Segmented Labor Force

At the turn of the century, America was on the verge of becoming a major industrial power. Immense and untapped resources lay to the west, and their exploitation would shape industrial capitalism in America. The emergence of industry in the West was, however, very different from that which had been developed in other parts of the United States. In California it was agribusiness, and in Texas a combination of extract mining and agribusiness. These industries relied on a large supply of cheap labor in order for them to be profitable. In Texas, three major historical events took place that secured such a labor force, and would shape a system of racial stratification throughout the republic.

The three historical events that shaped racial stratification throughout Texas are central to Barrera's (1979) study of social inequality: the Mexican–American War, the displacement of the indigenous population from their land, and the emergence of a segmented labor force.

The Yellow Rose, pages 11–20

The Mexican–American War[1]

The Mexican–American War accentuated the intense competition between Mexicans and Anglos. Mexican officials had become suspicious of the growing number of Americans in Texas. Moreover, the attempts of two American presidents, John Quincy Adams and Andrew Jackson, to purchase Texas from Mexico intensified these suspicions.[2]

There were several important roots to the tense relations between Mexico and the United States: the concept of Manifest Destiny, the economic value of the Rio Grande, and U.S. cotton interests. As an ideology, Manifest Destiny provided U.S. leadership a justification for their westward expansion and the desire to dominate North America. Manifest Destiny stressed that it was America's destiny to take control of the North American continent because it was a superior nation and thus entitled to have such control. It was arrogance of the first magnitude. This dominant sentiment is captured in the following statement by Ashbee Smith, a former secretary of state for the Texas Republic in 1848, in which he described the Mexican war as "part of a mission, of the destiny allotted to the Anglo-Saxon race... to civilize, to Americanize this continent" (as cited in Montejano 1992, p. 24).

A second factor lay in economics. Indeed, Montejano (1992) argues that the Rio Grande was potentially a source of much wealth because it connected Santa Fe, New Mexico to Chihuahua, Mexico and would open a clear path for worldwide trade. But just as important was the port of Matamoros, where "silver bullion, lead, wool hides, and beef talon" (Montejano 1992, p. 16) all passed through that port city. Thus, the Rio Grande, seemed to many American businessmen in Texas, a potential point of trading with the rest of the world.

Finally, there were U.S. cotton interests and the desire by some American businessmen to import more slaves for cotton production, as well as the interests of Anglos in Texas to engage in free trade with the United States (Meier & Rivera, 1972). Mexico, however, had abolished slavery and since Texas was part of Mexico's territory, it was subject to Mexico's laws and policies. Such a fact did not impede U.S. imperialism.

The Mexican–American War began in 1846 and ended with the signing of the Treaty of Guadalupe Hidalgo in 1848. With the signing of that treaty, the United States acquired a sizeable piece of property. Indeed, the land under consideration now comprises the states of California, New Mexico, Arizona, Nevada, Utah, part of Colorado, and, of course, Texas.

The war was not positively viewed by all American leaders. Later in life, Ulysses S. Grant expressed his deep shame about the war:

> With a soldier the flag is paramount... I know the struggle with my conscience during the Mexican war. I have never altogether forgiven myself for going into that. I had very strong opinions on the subject. I do not think there was ever a more wicked war than that waged by the United States on Mexico. I thought so at the time, when I was a youngster, only I had not moral courage enough to resign. I had taken an oath to serve eight years, unless sooner discharged, and I considered my supreme duty was to my flag. I had a horror of the Mexican war, and I have always believed that it was on our part most unjust. The wickedness was not in the way our soldiers conducted it, but in the conduct of our government in declaring war. The troops behaved well in Mexico, and the government acted handsomely about the peace. We had no claim on Mexico. Texas had no claim beyond the Nueces River, and yet we pushed on to the Rio Grande and crossed it. I am always ashamed of my country when I think of that invasion. (as quoted in Young, 2002, pp. 376–377).

Displacement of the Indigenous Population From the Land

The war led to three important factors that created a system of racial stratification in Fabens.[3] The first factor was the displacement of Mexicans from their land, and Mexicans who remained in Texas were now under U.S. law. What is noteworthy here is that Article X of the Treaty of Guadalupe Hidalgo was removed from the treaty. The article stated that land grants would be honored by the U.S. government. Its absence from the treaty would allow unscrupulous rent-seeking individuals to remove the native population from their lands. In Fabens, the displacement of the native populace from their land occurred both legally and illegally. Legally, individuals (primarily Anglos) who coveted a piece of land would lobby local officials and demand that small farmers pay their delinquent taxes. For many of the original inhabitants, paying taxes was unheard of and, besides, they had no money with which to pay such rents. Consequently, they were required to either leave the land or sell it at substantially reduced prices in order to pay their taxes. One example involved a judge of the district court colluding with big farmers in acquiring land for them and himself.

Land was also acquired illegally. J. P. Miller, a big farmer, who fenced in 25 acres of land that belonged to one of the original Mexican inhabitants and then "run him off," according to one Fabens informant. Further downstream, where there had been less Anglo power, resistance by Mexicans was stronger and Anglo farmers used greater force in achieving their goals. In 1917, for instance, Jesus Nunez, an old resident, was driven off his land by a land investment company, "They burned down his buildings, tore down his fences. He died in the county poor house," recalled one elderly informant.

In Fabens, several historical events fall into this category: the Elephant Butte Dam project, the Salt War, and the emergence of big farming. Why and how was such displacement tied to a race based stratification system? There are at least two ways land displacement affected the labor status of Mexican Americans. To begin with, it created a large labor force needed in the area as it was moving toward large agribusiness. As unattached persons in need of a wage in order to support themselves, Mexican Americans became paid laborers rather than small, independent farmers. This particular phenomena was not new, as it was practiced in England, and noted by Marx in Das Kapital:

> The prelude to the revolution that laid the foundation of the Capitalist mode of production was played out in the last third of the fifteenth century and the first few decades of the sixteenth. A mass of 'free' and unattached proletarians was hurled onto the labour market by the dissolution of the bands of feudal retainers (Marx, 1887/1995, p. 510)

The Elephant Butte Dam Project

The Elephant Butte Dam project is significant for two reasons. First, it opened the way for big farming in Fabens. A reliable source of water made the surrounding land a haven for increased agricultural production. However, the emergence of big farming in Fabens initiated conflict between big farmers and small land-owning Mexicans. It also transformed Mexicans from a small, rural peasantry to a large and cheap source of menial labor. Second, the project was instrumental in a tightly interwoven relationships among certain Anglo businessmen who would control the sale of property in the Fabens community and would figure prominently in the early history of the community.

The Salt War

The El Paso Salt War fiasco highlighted Mexican–Anglo power differentials and heightened racial tensions in the Fabens community. Anglos hoping to get rich with the coming of the railroads poured into Fabens. Among the new migrants was Charles Howard, a Missouri lawyer and Democrat who had been a Lieutenant in the Confederate Army.[4]

About ninety miles east of El Paso were some large salt deposits that were freely available to anyone. Howard obtained a certificate to the land

and served notice that the salt would, from then on, be sold. When two Mexicans said they would go for salt any time they wished, Howard had them arrested. A group of 40 to 50 armed men released the two Mexicans and arrested both Howard and a county judge who had refused to imprison Howard (Mills, 1962, p. 151).

Louis Cardis and Antonio Borjis arranged for Howard to be released in exchange for his signing a statement that he would "forget all that had passed," leave the region permanently and immediately, leave the question of the salt deposits up to the courts, and give $12,000 bond to prove his good faith. Howard left and went to Mesilla, New Mexico where he telegrammed the governor of Texas about the danger of an invasion from Mexico. A month later Howard returned to El Paso and killed Louis Cardis. Howard turned himself in to the local sheriff, and spent very little time in jail. After his release he and a group of strongmen, along with a detachment of Texas Rangers, set out for San Elizario to seize a load of salt. Upon their arrival, they were met by a large group of armed men and sought refuge in a nearby adobe building. In the ensuing gun battle, Howard's agent, Ellis, and a Texas Ranger were killed. Eventually, the rangers surrendered, were disarmed, and set free. Howard, Atkinson, and McBride were summarily executed (Sonnichsen, 1968).

The Salt War was investigated by a congressional committee in 1878, and the next year Fort Bliss was reestablished. A grand jury indicted six men as the ringleaders, and offered rewards for their capture. They were never caught. Some of Fabens' elderly citizens recalled that the El Paso Salt War contributed to increased racial tension in the community.

The Franklin Canal

When the Franklin Canal in Fabens was completed in 1916, rich farmers began buying large tracts of land in the surrounding community. The pressure brought on by big farmers on smaller ones included working with the local government in demanding that small farmers pay neglected taxes, use of the legal system to acquire land, and the enclosure system used so well in 19th century England.

Segmented Labor Force

A segmented labor force was another factor contributing to racial stratification in Fabens. Historians have argued that the rapid economic expansion the United States was undergoing at the turn of the century affected the lives of Mexicans in the Southwest (Barrera, 1979; Garcia, 1981). Rapid economic expansion occurred in such industries as extract mining, railroad building, and in agriculture.

The need, then, was for a large cadre of cheap unskilled labor. Mexicans who had recently been displaced from their land and a large immigrant population from Mexico filled that need.

Accounts related to this massive transformation of the Fabens community are sparse, and putting together a coherent narrative depends on two sources: Fabens history and data from the surrounding communities. Both sources should provide us with an account of what transpired in Fabens. González (1967) writes:

> Most of these dispossessed persons became part of the farm labor force, whose ranks were swelled considerably by immigration from Mexico. (p. 52)

Indeed, immigration contributed to the segmented labor force because new arrivals from Mexico, being unattached to both the land and the community, accepted inferior jobs and wages.

And what is a segmented labor force? A segmented labor force is based on the notion of differentiation among workers and that such differentiation is associated with different work experiences (see Averitt, 1968; Baran & Sweezy, 1966; Dickens & Lang, 1993; Doeringer & Piore, 1972; Piore, 1972; Reich, Gordon, & Edwards, 1973). For example, different wages, working conditions, opportunities for advancement, and safety.

A segmented labor force is tied to an unanticipated change in capitalism. Marx and others had expected capitalism to run its course and be replaced by another production system, but it never happened. Instead, competitive capitalism was replaced by monopoly capitalism, which is the natural result of hyper competition. That is, in order to maximize profits, eliminate your competition. Monopoly capitalism is a system where industry is controlled by a few. In such a system, there are two labor markets: one is tied to the *core* economy, and the other to its *periphery*. Monopoly capitalism emerged from the unsettling practices and outcomes from competitive capitalism, with its routine recessions and depressions (See Baran & Sweezy, 1966).

There are at least five traits of a secondary labor market (SLM). First, SLMs are organized around structures and their own organization rather than the traits of workers. Second, there is some mobility in SLMs, but it is within, rather than between, types of jobs. Third, workers' behaviors are the outcome of interactions between ideology, family, the organization of work, neighborhoods, and so forth. Fourth, discrimination is a trait of SLMs, but its elimination will not eliminate poverty or underemployment. Finally, SLMs are symbolic, emphasizing the dialectical tension between competing symbols, such as perfect competition versus monopoly (Harrison & Sum, 1979).

Jobs in the core sector pay well, are organized by rational policies, have opportunities for advancement, are safe, and require skilled labor. Jobs in the periphery sector are the exact opposite. In Fabens, Mexican Americans were in periphery jobs.

A disproportionate number of Mexicans in low paying, unskilled jobs would qualify as a segmented labor force. These were jobs in which Mexicans were also exploited as a reserve or buffer labor force (Barrera, 1979). Mario Garcia (1981) also presents data that exhibit considerable occupational segregation in nearby El Paso. Garcia found that Mexican workers were highly concentrated in labor and service jobs from 1900 to 1940. Indeed, from 1900 to 1940, both occupational categories accounted for about 60% of the Spanish surnamed labor force in El Paso. As a second measure of occupational segmentation, indices of dissimilarity (D) were computed. The index ranges from 0 to 100: 0 being no segmentation and 100 being complete segmentation. In 1900, the index was 49.63 and by 1940 it declined to 36.65. Thus, though there was some decline in occupational segregation, it remained at a high level, as there needed to be a 36% redistribution of Anglos and Spanish speakers for both groups to be equally distributed across occupations.

I used data for the years 1960 and 1970 decennial census in looking at the occupational distributions for both Mexican Americans and non-Hispanics age 16–64 in the labor force in Texas. Results are interesting and point out several interesting stories (see Figure 3.1).

To begin with, in 1960 the largest percentage of Mexican-American workers were located in craft occupation. Indeed, their percentage was greater than that of non-Hispanic workers: 27.4 v. 24.0. Second, the next two occupations with large percentages of the Mexican-American labor force in Texas were farm occupations (14.5%), and service occupations (10.2%). Distributions changed by 1970.

In 1970, the top three occupations for Mexican-American workers were craft (29.3%), operatives (16.2%), and service jobs (12.2%).

Interestingly, these results point out that there was some upward job mobility among Mexican-American workers from 1960 to 1970. Of particular interest were movement into professional occupations, and the increase in craft jobs. Were these patterns observed in Fabens?

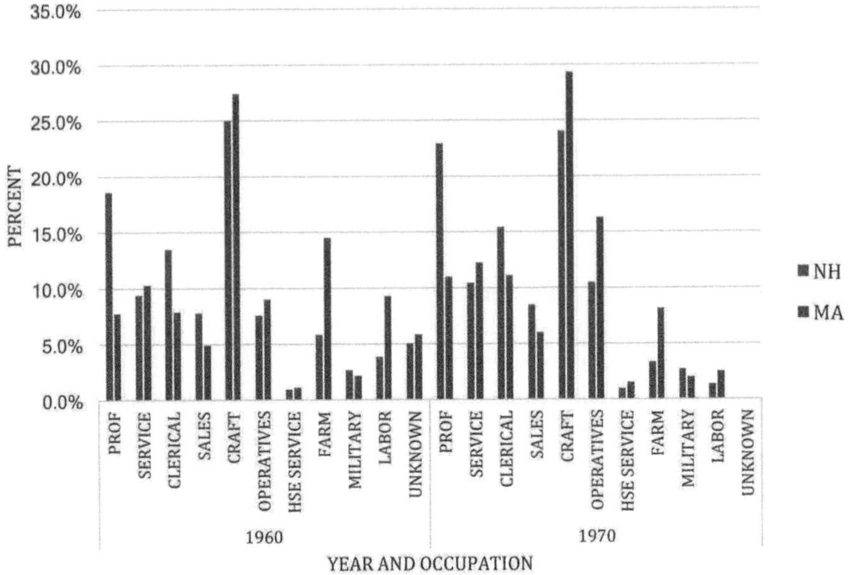

Figure 3.1 Occupational distribution among non-Hispanics and Mexican American workers, Age 16+, 1960 and 1970. *Source*: Ruggles et al. (2017).

Segmented labor markets are also characterized by differential wages to persons doing the same job. In El Paso several studies revealed that Mexican workers received lower wages than Anglos (see Garcia, 1981, pp. 88–96). Indeed, two wage structures existed in El Paso: one for Anglos and another for Mexicans. While I do not have data on wage differentials for Fabens at this early point in its history, I assume that a similar wage structure was in place in Fabens because it is located in El Paso County. Moreover, a description of labor market distributions in Texas would also be informative. My assumption is such a distribution would be mirrored in Fabens. Figure 3.2 displays the distribution of workers in Texas by *Good*, *Average*, and *Poor* jobs based on the Duncan socioeconomic index (SEI), for the years 1850 to 1900.[5]

Basically, these data confirm the notion that Mexican Americans in Texas were overwhelmingly in bad jobs, and a small percentage were actually in good jobs. Thus, in 1850, 9.7% of non-Hispanics age 16–64 who were in the labor force were in poor jobs; in contrast, 44.7% of Mexican Americans were in poor jobs. By 1900, the percentages in poor jobs were 34.4% versus 68.3%.

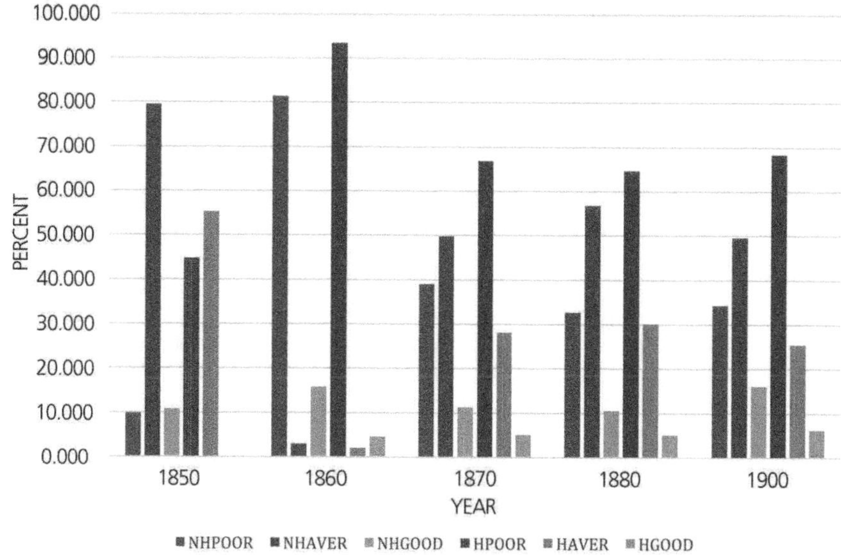

Figure 3.2 Good and bad jobs by non-Hispanics and Mexican Americans in Texas, 1850–1900.

Notes

1. In a somewhat humorous statement, Mexican President Perfirio Diaz said, "Poor Mexico, so far from God, so close to the United States."
2. There were at least two reasons why the United States moved into the Southwest. First, there was the anxiety of movement into the area by foreign powers, especially England (Billington, 1974). Second, there was the American economy (North, 1966). On the one hand, England was making great efforts to limit America's hold on the North American continent because it recognized America as a formidable competitor. For instance, England was helping the Mexican government in its attempt to retain its northern provinces. On the other hand, starting around 1830, the United States experienced a major increase in the value of its export trade. The funds that were realized from this trade were crucial in the economic development of the United States. Cotton was the most important of these export trade goods. Thus, with the increased value of cotton came the need for land acquisition, and the southwest became the logical choice.
3. Joan Moore and Alfredo Cuellar (1970) points out that the conquest of Mexican Americans did not follow a common pattern: Conquest in New Mexico followed a *classic colonialism* pattern, *economic colonialism* occurred in California, and *conflict colonialism* happened in Texas. And, given the extreme history of violence in Texas, it is not surprising that an extreme form of racial stratification evolved in that state. Also, for an excellent discussion of racial inequality

in the southwest see Barrera (1979, Chapters 1–3, & 7). Barrera's work, I believe, is useful for two reasons. First, he discusses the importance of two historical processes in shaping racial inequality: conquest and land displacement, and second, he attempts to construct a theory of racial inequality.

4. Howard, however, was a reckless soul.

> For any man, no matter how friendly he was with the Mexicans, to have attempted this would have been dangerous, but for Howard, who was not popular and who had a good many of the undesirable traits of a bully, to undertake it was simply foolhardy and hazardous.
>
> The land on which the lakes are located was public and it was open . . . to any man who had enough scip in his possession to cover it . . . In the name of his father-in-law, Major George B. Zimpleman (an Austin Banker, soldier, and financier), he took up the land and as soon as the certificates of title were in his hands he served notice on the Mexican people on both sides of the river that thereafter salt would be sold at so much a fanega (in 1877). (White, 1924, p. 116)

5. Jobs were determined by, first, computing one-half of the standard deviation of SEI scores for each year. Good jobs were the mean score plus one half of the standard deviation. Average jobs were those within the plus/minus of the mean SEI scores, and poor jobs were jobs less than the mean SEI minus one half of the standard deviation. Data were computed for workers age 16–64, in the labor force.

4

Land, Economics, and Labor

The Emergence of the Chicano Working Class

In 1900, the United States was in the early stages of industrializing. The American Civil War had ended 35 years earlier, and the Confederate states were rebuilding. Texas, as a member of the Confederacy, was also rebuilding and continuing its practices of segregating, and excluding Blacks and Mexican Americans. In this chapter, I describe three major factors that not only transformed Fabens, but directly affected the emergence of the Mexican-American middle class: struggles over land, the economic environment, and labor unrest.

Land Displacement of the Mexican Population

Water was a premium in the Fabens area and the fact that it was not plentiful was a major impediment to large farming in the area. This all changed with the completion of the Franklin Canal in 1916. The completion of the canal not only made water plentiful, but attracted rich farmers like Lee Moore to the area, and set in motion years of hostile relationships between

The Yellow Rose, pages 21–40

large and small farmers over property rights. Indeed, the pressure brought to bear on small farmers by wealthy men to relinquish their lands was significant and at times violent. A key factor in the equation was the fact that the majority of small farmers were Mexican Americans.

There is a price to pay for being an American. Paying taxes on one's land was unheard of before Anglo arrival. Few of the older Mexican-American residents had actually paid taxes on their land; in fact, the idea of land taxes escaped many of the older residents entirely. But the annexation of Texas to the Union brought about many changes, and paying taxes on one's land was one such change.

As the demand for land intensified, the Anglo-controlled county government took a significant role in displacing Mexican Americans from their land in Fabens. For example, when a wealthy landowner wanted to own an adjacent piece of property, he would place great pressure on county officials to demand immediate payment of back taxes from the owner of the property in question. The small farmer would either sell his land in order to pay the tax debt, or he would simply abandon the land and move elsewhere. The opportunity for corruption was great and Fabens' folklore has it that the judge of the district court worked in collaboration with big farmers in redistributing land. Moreover, the judge was himself able to acquire large portions of land throughout the valley as his own reward.

As older farmers died, their heirs, feeling less attached to the land, often sold the property and moved to nearby cities, such as El Paso. One elderly respondent reported that a young man traded his deceased father's farm for a Dodge Roadster. In another incident the Federico Arroyo and Jesus Amaya farms were reportedly sold at an exceedingly low price by their heirs.

Lawyers were in particularly advantageous positions to claim land either through tax proceedings or estate litigations. One long-time Fabens resident recalled that when Don Luciano Lopez died, his sons argued over their shares of his estate and hired a lawyer to settle the matter. The lawyer offered an informant $100 to swear in court that the widow was *non compos mentis*, after which an administrator would be named "and the court would take it from there." The informant not only refused but warned the sons. The widow died shortly thereafter and the case continued in court for years, with the youngest son temporarily running the farm as an administrator. The lawyer finally claimed a large part of the estate; the sons, nearly ruined, sold the land to pay their debts and eventually left town.

Small landowners resisting pressures brought about by large farm owners, were subjected to more direct methods. One such method was the enclosure system which was successfully used by 19th century British agricultural expansionists (see Marx, 1867/1990, Vol. 1, Chapter 27; Overton, 1996; Thompson, 1963; Turner, 1984).[1] In the enclosure method, land surrounding an intransigent small farmer would be bought up. The small farmer would then be fenced in and watch the value of his land substantially diminish when his access to water had been cut off. Selling land was his only recourse—and at a significantly lower price, of course. There were two important consequences of the enclosure system as stated by Marx (1887/1990) and by Overton (1996). First, land was transformed from subsistence use, to be used for profit making by larger farmers. Second, it transformed the landed peasantry into wage laborers. Indeed, Overton (1996) argues that the increased supply of labor was a major factor in the emergence of the industrial revolution.

Anglos who owned small farms met a similar fate:

> We had the original titles—recorded in El Paso in the County Record Office. I took in the original titles when the Boundary Commission came down to straighten out the border, the treaty specified that any chunk of land that would be cut off [by straightening the river course] would be under the International Boundary Commission. Mexico named it in 1908 but it [the Commission] was dissolved before it got started [in the 1910 Revolution]. When the U.S. Commission came in 1908, Boundary Commissioner Corbin told my dad to stay, he had the only title... in 1916... these land grabbers didn't stop at anything... burned their houses down, ripped up fences, some of them were killed... these people were scared. He [the father] had to go to the hospital; we [the sons] all went to war... He came back a month later—they'd already jumped the place and he never could get them off... [It was] some of those real estate muscle men—"killers" is what they were called in those days. They tried the case in the district court in El Paso and they dispossessed him legally. They had no jurisdiction because it had not been decided whether it was United States or Mexican land.

The organizations most active in displacing small famers were the McElroy Investment Company, the Newman Investment Company, and the W. F. Payne Investment Company.

Data on the percent of the Texas population residing on farms from 1850 to 1970 are displayed in Figure 4.1.

My hypothesis is that over time, the share of the Mexican population residing on farms would decline as many began losing their land to larger, Anglo farmers. Data are for the state of Texas, but I am assuming that Mexican Americans in Fabens suffered the same fate. Data in Figure 4.1 confirms my hypothesis. In 1850, 52% of Mexican Americans in Texas lived on farms, and 72% of Anglos lived on farms. By 1900, the Mexican American and Anglo percentages living on farms were 23% and 65%, respectively.

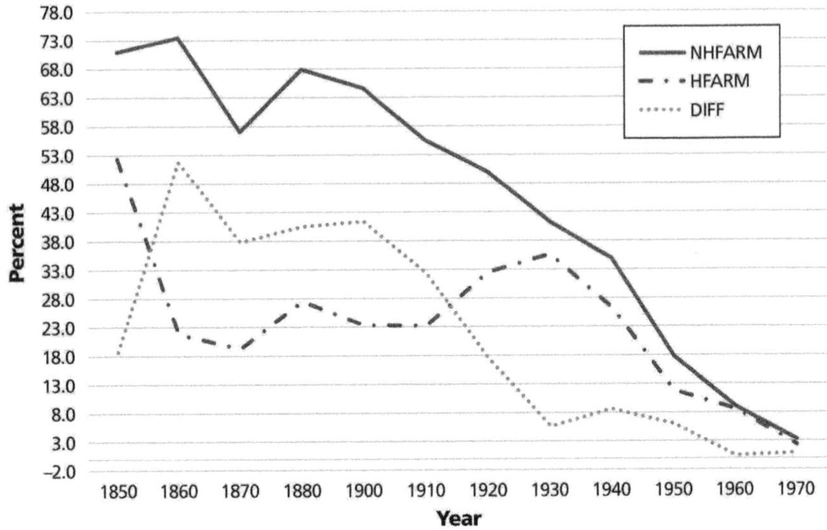

Figure 4.1 Percent of population on farms in Texas, 1850–1970.

In 1970 (data refer to the previous year, 1969, the year the Fabens survey was conducted), the Mexican American and Anglo percentages residing on farms dramatically declined and the percentages were nearly equal: 2.3% and 3.3%, respectively. What these data tend to exhibit is the urbanization of the Texas population.

A significant offshoot of displacing small farmers was to drive them into the labor force—that is, a large cadre of potentially cheap labor who had experience working on farms.

Most of these displaced persons became part of the farm labor population, whose ranks considerably swelled by immigration from Mexico (González, 1967, p. 52).

The long, bitter resistance of the Fabens citizenry, as with the population down river from Fabens, and the people of "the Island between 1877 and 1893," can be linked to two very different kinds of social organizations. On the one hand, there was the Mexican hand-to-mouth peasant economy and, on the other hand, a rural Anglo community, Anglo farmers—and the presence of Federal troops. At times, these conflicting lifestyles gave way to violence.

These factors, along with the influx of large numbers of people from Guadalupe who had no attachment to the land or to the community surrounding Fabens, probably effectively neutralized any potential for organized resistance by the original landowners. Newcomers to Fabens accepted subservient roles in the Anglo–capitalist system, represented by the railroad, big farmers, and El Paso markets, since it provided them with the security and material well-being not available to them in Mexico.

Rich Mexicans émigrés like Marciano Rey also may have helped mediate the takeover process. Additionally, the courts and available lawyers were also part of an encroaching system that appeared to operate in fundamental sympathy, if not in active conspiracy, with new landowners. As one survivor of the original peasant families recalls:

> Nobody said anything or was angered, because... nobody had bought anything or paid taxes. They [big farmers] bought it in El Paso, in the courts—here nobody knows whose it was, somebody would say it was his.

Objections from the majority Mexican population, who had come from Mexico to improve their economic status, became less likely as new landowners established themselves in a social system of their own making. Newcomers came to work by clearing the land and preparing it for cultivation. Starting with the construction of the branches of the main irrigation canal in 1915, and continuing at least through 1918, Mexicans worked with shovels, hatchets, and horse teams, clearing and levelling land, and hauling away wood and brush.

Employment also increased immediately as land was cleared and in need of cultivating. The desperate need for work and sustenance halted the possibility of any resistance by Mexican workers.

Cotton Farming

During World War I, cotton reached a price of 75 cents per pound. Since the early mission days, cotton had been grown on small plots of land by Mexicans. But it was the owners of large cotton farms in the Imperial Valley, California, who recognized the potential of the Lower El Paso Valley as a place for growing cotton on a large scale, and as a major source of revenue. Such a business opportunity could not be ignored.

Jerome B. Dale and T. M. Berry bought 1,300 acres of uncultivated land that had once been the location of the Allison Farm in Tornillo. Louis J. Ivey, also of the Imperial Valley, bought some land and started the Iveydale farms. In 1917, Ivey settled in Fabens and hired large crews of Mexican laborers to clear the bosque and mesquite and build a cotton gin. In 1917, the land had not been adequately prepared and produced little cotton, but by 1918 a large cotton crop generated about two bales of cotton per acre.

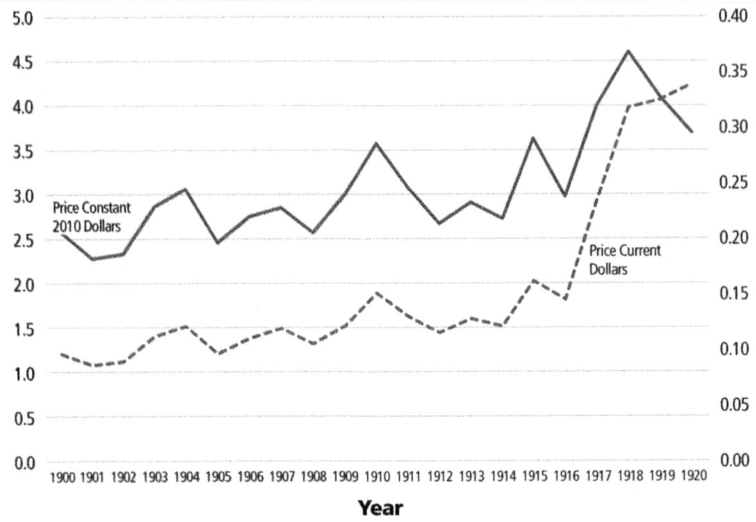

Figure 4.2 Price of raw cotton per pound (current values), 1900–1920. *Source:* Officer and Williamson (2019a).

By 1920 farmers from other parts of Texas, as well as from Mississippi, Oklahoma, and Arkansas who were moving into the Fabens area, began clearing the remaining wooded lands (Tenth Annual Cotton Festival Souvenir Program, 1968). Cotton was king.

In fact, cotton prices increased significantly from 1900 to 1920. Figure 4.2 displays the price of raw cotton per pound from 1900 to 1920. In 1900 the price of raw cotton per pound in current dollars was .096 cents, and by 1920 it had risen to .339 cents per pound in current dollars. Data in constant 2010 dollars also are displayed in Figure 4.2. The left axis is in constant 2010 dollars, while the right axis is the price of cotton in current dollars. Constant 2010 dollars gives us a better sense of the price of raw cotton from 1900 to 1920. In 1900, the price in constant 2010 dollars was 2.57 dollars per pound, and it rose to 3.69 dollars per pound by 1920. There was a clear economic reason for growing cotton, especially on large farms.

Labor Unrest

Among the newcomers to Fabens were several Slavs, including Tony Rancich. Some of the Slavs had been involved in a strike against the copper mining trust, including the famous strike against Phelps-Dodge Corporation in Arizona in June of 1917. In July, big business interests in Arizona and local citizens' war hysteria declared the strike to be "pro-German." This rise of nationalism subjected the strikers to assaults by vigilantes, guards, gunmen, and finally Federal troops when the Arizona mines were declared "war premises" by the Sabotage Act of 1918. At one point, 1,200 strikers and citizens, including many members of the International Workers of the World (which led the strike) and 179 Slavs, were loaded on a cattle train, kept there for 3 days without food in the desert and then 3 months in a stockade at Columbus, NM, without being charged (Renshaw, 1967, pp. 234–235). Upon their release in October 1917, several left the area and settled on farms in Fabens. Later the courts ruled that the actions by the Phelps-Dodge organization and Sheriff Wheeler were illegal. Wheeler was never prosecuted for his actions. In fact, he was in Europe fighting during WWI. Nonetheless, no one was prosecuted.

The development of large-scale cotton farming in Fabens was not entirely smooth. Profits for big farmers disappeared temporarily during a cotton market crash in 1920, when the price of cotton fell from 75 cents to 7 cents "with no buyers." One respondent noted, for workers,

> the escarda [cotton chopping or weeding] and the pisca [harvest] ended and meant the loss of four months of work. Then they [the farmers] used only those who lived on the farms all year... It has always been like this—work only for four months. There has never been work in the winter, only in the summer.

By this time, relative peace had returned to Chihuahua, and the majority of those who had left Mexico during the revolution gradually began returning home to Mexico, family by family. "Even though they could earn $0.75 to $1.00 per day, more than they could in Mexico, they didn't like it here." For many, the desire to get back to Mexico was a priority, and sacrifices were made to ensure their journey. For example, a magazine report in 1922 described the plight of over 200 Mexican workers who were stranded in Juarez after having worked in the El Paso Valley. The workers were without jobs or money and were asking for protection and assistance in returning to Mexico.

While many workers moved to Mexico, some apparently were satisfied with moving back and forth, depending on the season and on the political and economic conditions on either side of the border. The cost of living, however, was relatively low, and while most of the original immigrants returned home, many newcomers were attracted to the seasonal cotton farming jobs. These workers also included Blacks, lower-class White ethnics, and displaced young males from the interior of Mexico. At the same time, there was an exodus of the younger generation from the older families in the

Fabens area which was probably spurred by the changing local culture, loss of year-round employment, and the competition from newcomers.

The Boom Years

Fabens appears to have settled down during the period of 1923–1926. Many older locals recalled the period as having the greatest prosperity. "There was a lot of work, and life was cheaper." Cotton, alfalfa, and milo maize profits led to increased wages—up to 10 cents an hour, or $7.50 for a normal 6-day work week. Workers with higher status jobs earned anywhere from $1.25 to $1.50 per day.[2] While farm workers lived in rows of small adobe houses built along the canals, the upper class farm owners, like W. A. Raws, and businessmen, like "Pappy Hendricks," First National Bank president, were able to build large homes either on their farms or across the tracks from the Mexican adobes of La Tortuga. There were other types of work available, such as fishing or trapping along the canals. Anglo-owned service stations were established, and Roy Reeder sold DeSoto and Plymouth cars.

A men's fraternal organization, the Cruz Azul [Blue Cross] was established in 1923. They appear not to have done charitable work, but to have made door-to-door collections to fund Fourth of July and Diez y Seis de Septiembre fiestas. It was about this time that Fabens was incorporated as a city, with an elected mayor. However, the attempt at setting up a formal democratic local government was abandoned within a year due to a lack of cooperation and, mainly, because it was impossible to levy taxes. The town eventually returned to its present unincorporated status.

A flood in 1925 or 1926 may have been responsible for some decline in the local economy. By 1925–1927, the expansion into new irrigable land had been completed. The Border Patrol was established in 1924, the border closed, and Mexicans without citizenship papers or a passport were expelled with increasing regularity. The economic boom in Fabens was coming to an end. Little did Fabens' citizens realize that impending national forces were to seal the end to its economic boom.

The Great Depression

As a result of several factors far beyond the borders of Fabens, the boom years in Fabens ended. Economic conditions began to falter during the Great Depression and reached its zenith in 1932. The Great Depression began in 1929 with the collapse of the stock market, and lasted until approximately 1938. Unemployment and poverty rates were high, and the Dow dropped like a lead balloon.

At its crest during the Great Depression, unemployment characterized one-quarter of the labor force. From 1925 to 1929, unemployment rates were in the single digits. In 1925, the unemployment rate stood at 4%, and dropped to 3.2% by 1929. From 1931 to 1940 it stayed at double digits.

Unemployment reached its zenith in 1933, at 25% before dropping to 14.6% by 1940 (see Figure 4.3).

A second measure of the dire situation brought on by the Great Depression was the drop in the gross domestic product. Keep in mind that the GDP is an indicator of the health of the U.S. economy. In 1929 (in millions of 2009 dollars), the GDP stood at 1,056,600, and by 1930 it declined to 966,700. By 1933, the United States' GDP had plunged to 778,300 before it started to rise again (see Figure 4.4).

A third measure was bank closings during the Great Depression. In 1925 there were 617 bank closings, and by 1929 closings rose slightly to 659. In 1930, the number of bank closings doubled to 1,350, and by 1933 there were 4,000 bank closings (see Figure 4.5).

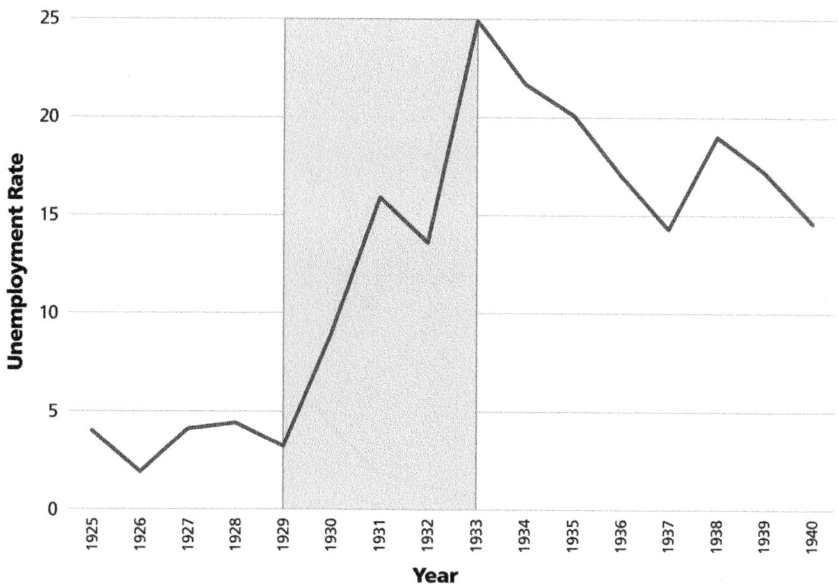

Figure 4.3 Unemployment rates during the Great Depression, 1925–1940. *Source*: BLS (www.bls.gov).

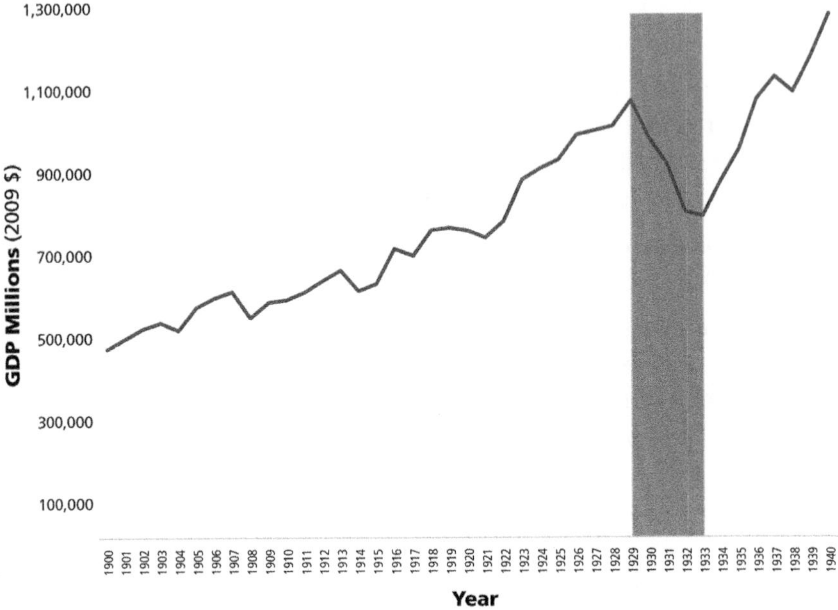

Figure 4.4 GDP in millions in 2009 dollars, 1900–1940. *Source:* Johnston and Williamson (2019).

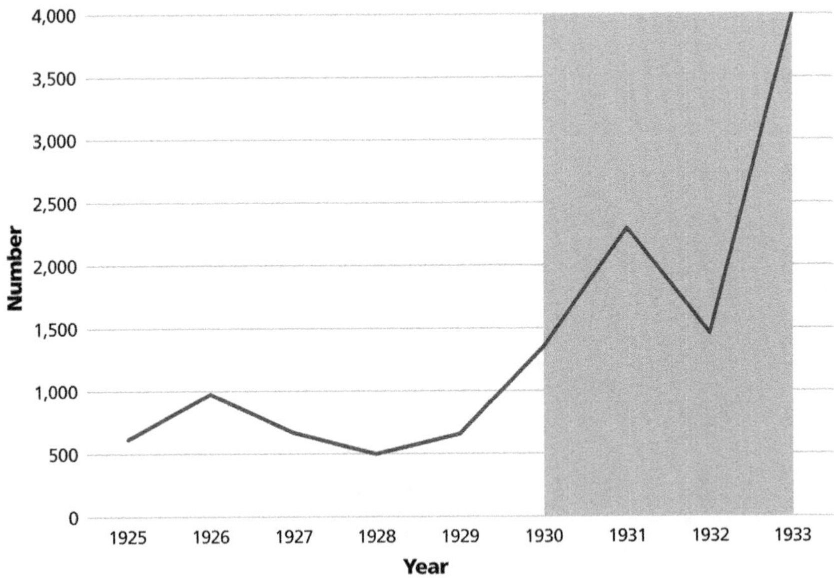

Figure 4.5 Bank closings, 1925–1933. *Source:* FRED (www.fred.stlouisfed.org).

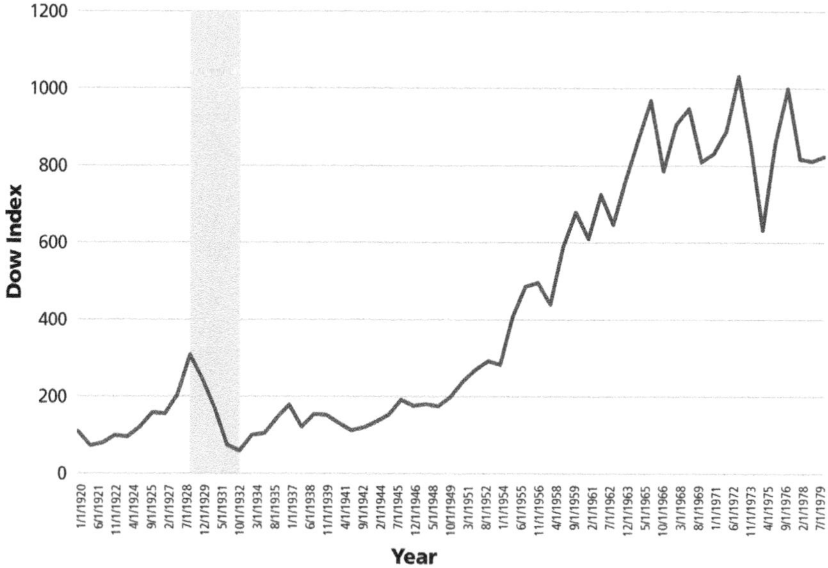

Figure 4.6 DOW industrial index, 1920–1980. *Source:* FRED (www.fred.stlouisfed.org).

As a fourth measure, I examined the Dow Industrial Index from 1920 to 1980. Data are displayed in Figure 4.6. The highlighted area in Figure 4.6 frames the 1929 to 1933 period of the Great Depression. The year 1933 appears to be the most serious year of the Depression. In 1929, the Dow Jones Industrial Average closed at 370.0, and by 1933, the Dow closed at 59.3, an 81% drop in the average from 1929 to 1933.

The Great Depression had varying effects on rural and urban areas. In rural areas, crops failed to grow, crop prices dropped (Alston, 1983; Perkins, 1969).[3] In addition, some farmers in the Plains states had to deal with the Dust Bowl, including those in the Northwestern part of Texas.

While the Great Depression contributed to the economic decline in Fabens, Fabens, like other farming areas, was hit by an earlier Depression of 1920–1921. In 1930, the average price of cotton in the Cotton Belt (including the El Paso Valley) had dropped to 29% of their value in 1927, and wages for cotton pickers were only 54% of what they had been in 1927. By 1931, cotton prices had fallen to 28%, and wages to 37%, of their levels in 1927. In the next 3 years farm owners were able to do better, and prices went up to 61% of their 1927 levels. Wages, in 1930, were 53% of wages in 1927 and did not catch up until 1936. Nationally, the wage situation was a bit different. Figure 4.7 displays nominal hourly wages for the years 1925 to

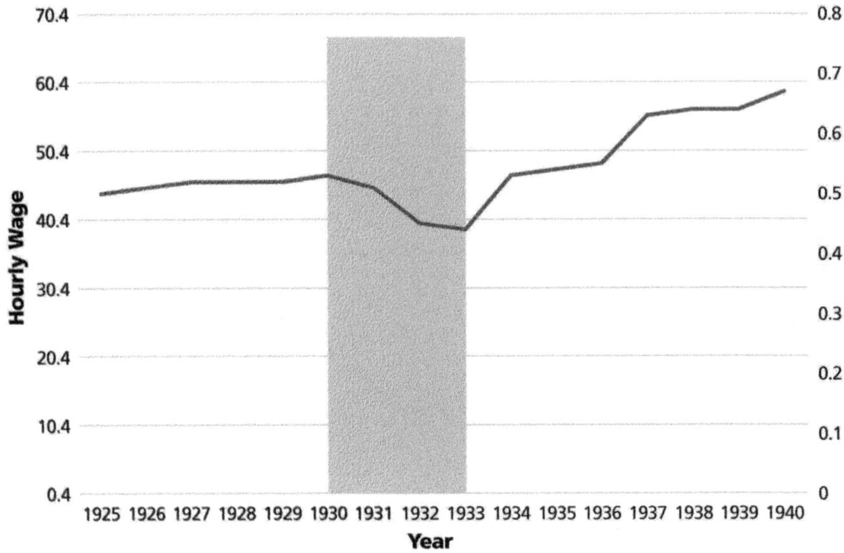

Figure 4.7 Nominal hourly wages among production workers in the United States, 1925–1940. Source: Officer and Williamson (2019b).

1940. As can be seen, there is a decline, but the decline is greatest in 1933, when the average hourly wage dropped to 44 cents.

Needless to say, the economic situation exerted tremendous strain on labor relations. In 1930, the largest, most highly organized strike in the El Paso Valley took place. The most successful strike, however, occurred in 1934 when cotton prices rose to their highest level since 1929; wages, however, were still quite low. The strike was successful because it was clear to most that farmers were capable of paying higher wages (Ahearn, 1945).

Increased agricultural mechanization in the Fabens area was a second factor contributing to its economic decline. Increased mechanization meant fewer jobs, therefore, less money in the Fabens economy.

A third factor was the flow of Mexican workers over the border, which had already resulted in high unemployment and the departure of large numbers of individuals from Fabens as early as 1922. Although immigration had begun in the 1890s, most came around 1900, when there were 71,062 immigrants, and 1930, when there were 683,681 people of Mexican origin in Texas. The biggest waves were during World War I, and again after the war (McWilliams, 1948/1990).

A fourth factor was ethnic conflict. The conflict between Anglos and Mexican Americans helped Anglo farm owners exploit Mexican workers, and destroy any attempts at unionization. Middle-class and working-class Anglos were not likely to object to such exploitation. Racism in the community effectively stopped workers from organizing against large farming interests that might have improved their economic status.

> When Mexican sheep-shearers went on strike in West Texas in 1934, one of the sheepmen made a speech in which he said: "We are a pretty poor bunch of white men if we are going to sit here and let a bunch of Mexicans tell us what to do." In 1933 a fifty-car caravan of Mexican workers, members of the Association de Jornaleros, paraded the length of the Lower Rio Grande Valley in protest against anti-union activity... With scarcely an exception, every strike in which Mexicans participated in the borderlands in the thirties was broken by the use of violence and was followed by deportations. In most of these strikes, Mexican workers stood alone, that is, they were not supported by organized labor, for their organizations, for the most part, were affiliated neither with the CIO or the AFL. (McWilliams, 1961, p. 194)

When the Depression came to Texas, many of those who had left to work elsewhere returned to their families. In Fabens, passing trains carried many displaced White and Black workers and families looking for work. When the train stopped, many got off and panhandled for money around the station. Work was available to most people for only 1, 2, or 3 days a week, and for 10 hours a day. A day's pay was 75 cents or even 60 cents. "The hunger was killing us. We ate one or two times a day... Another year of Hoover and we would have had a civil war—we would have had to kill him" recalls an older Mexican worker. A middle-class Anglo agreed in his own way: "I believe the country was on the verge of a revolution. They were getting desperate, ready to listen to anybody."

Another Anglo worker recalls,

> At one time here in this valley, there were nothing but peon labor. They paid them so little and sold so high in the commissaries... The foreman generally went around on horseback with a six-shooter, Winchester, or shotgun—telling you to get off, that included salesmen... The houses were nothing but shacks, no accommodations whatsoever, sometimes they camped under a tree and worked from sunrise to sunset and you had to buy everything from the commissary. They robbed them blind—charged them two to five times what you'd pay anywhere else... In most cases [this applied to] the ones living on the farm. They had to get up and go to work any time that they were called. None of them got overtime for anything—you were lucky to get straight time, and you wouldn't get it on the majority of the ranches. About 75% couldn't pay the commissary and at that time food was cheap, but they charged so much, they wouldn't let them leave the farm and wouldn't let

> nobody come in and move them off... Some of the farmers were not even paying them anything, just feeding them.

Labor discontent increased as farmers began cutting pay, made less work available, and demanded longer working hours. In 1929 or 1930, about 100 farm workers "had a little march down Main Street... It wasn't really a strike. It was a demonstration for more pay." One of the organizers recalled:

> Well, at one time we had the whole valley—all of El Paso County—we went to all of the little towns. We held meetings and got them to organize. That's the only time the laborers in this part of the county got organized. From town to town we'd get them to organize their town—after we talked to them the one's we'd consider capable would form a committee, three on a committee. Ysleta, then Socorro, San Elizario, Fabens, Ft. Hancock, McNary, Camp Ninety—all in 1929... It was a mutual organization for self-defense and self-preservation. Never a name, "Farm Union" is what we referred to it as—"La Union Agricola." If we held a meeting they'd [the local police] come and break it up and threaten us... The law, they were in favor of the farmers—they were being paid by the farmers to make it rough for us... We wasn't breaking the law. Down at the Malone Ranch they shot a hole through my windshield, that was about '30... We didn't have the funds to carry on, the people couldn't hold out any longer, so we lost the strike. We did it with no other purpose than to try to help the people of the community. We didn't call it off—by the end of December, it went to pieces... I had to leave the county, I went to Arizona, New Mexico, California;... he [Dave Cresswell] went to Douglas, Arizona, he's still there. Gilberto died in 1935. I couldn't get no work.

Another, more militant, strike took place in 1934 during the cotton harvest. "Everybody treated everyone equal," recalled a respondent. "We all respected those who knew how to talk... It wasn't organized." One striker recalls the militancy:

> We guarded all the bridges here, but they came across at night from Ft. Hancock and El Paso. We would grab them off the ranches and throw them out. We didn't beat them up or hurt them. They hid or ran when we came, just like from the Immigration...

The Roosevelt administration brought the New Deal and its legislation on farming, employment, and welfare which affected the people of Fabens. Aid to farm owners began under the Agricultural Adjustment Act in 1933; the success of the following year's strike was linked to the farmers' increased ability to raise wages. Another consequence was a sharp increase in employment, resulting in Mexicans crossing the border again for work. The period of strikes during the Depression was a time of intense struggles between rich

Anglo farmers (with the aid of the local police) and the Mexican/Mexican-American workers (but included Whites and Blacks). Workers were assisted by at least some Mexican-American small businessmen, represented by the Carbajals (Fabens inhabitants), and the Border Patrol guards, who lived in the Fabens community and were not controlled by big farmers.

Recovery, World War II and the Postwar Period

> *By 1935–1936 conditions had improved to the extent that hunger was for the most part eliminated, partly through direct relief to provide food, clothing, and rent money.*
>
> —Fabens informant

A Civilian Conservation Corps (CCC) camp northeast of Fabens, one of several in the Valley, housed young men employed in road work, flood control construction, and reclamation projects. Young women were sent to be trained in El Paso in a program of the Federal Emergency Relief Administration. The most important organization was the *Works Progress Administration* (WPA) which started in 1936 and employed large numbers of men from all areas of the Valley to work on a variety of public works projects. The projects included cutting wood, quarrying and crushing rock in the hills to the north for road construction, and for construction at Fort Bliss near El Paso.

The Boundary Commission supervised a WPA project in an attempt to straighten out the course of the Rio Grande, hiring workers at $2 per day—with no compensation for workers if they were injured. Workers burned brush, grubbed out trees, and shoveled earth before bulldozers were called upon to do the final, large-scale clearing and preparation of the channel. The river was "rectified" to its present course in 1937. Wages on the projects reached a high of about $4 to $5 per day by the end of the decade (Montgomery, 1987).

Workers in the Fabens were never to live as they had during the halcyon years of the 1920s based on the production of cotton. A major trend was occurring that would replace workers—the machine. Moreover, most of the federal policies aimed at improving the economic problems facing farming, in reality benefited farmers and did little to improve the economic status of farmworkers. The 1933 Agricultural Adjustment Act began aid to farmers, and was replaced in 1936 by the Soil Conservation and Domestic Allotment Act, when the former was declared unconstitutional:

> Between 1932 and 1940, government payments to the farmers totaled 3.8 billion dollars and in 1939 farm benefit payments amounted to 807 million dollars. Doubtless, farm laborers benefited indirectly by the agricultural

> program but it was the farmers not they who were intended to be the main beneficiaries of the policy . . . They were specifically excluded from the Wagner Act, the Federal Social Security Act, and the Wage-Hour Act. No state included them in its Unemployment Insurance plan. And practically all the states, upon inauguration of their Workmen's Compensation Laws, neglected to cover farm laborers (Ahearn, 1945, p. 168).

Farm workers' wages, as a result, dropped to one fourth of the wages being earned by factory workers, compared to being two thirds of factory workers' wages in the period 1910–1914. Low wages and high unemployment worked in conjunction in making the lower El Paso Valley an undesirable place for farm work. "Back in 1939," recalled one farm worker in 1966, "I travel[ed] to West Texas, to pick cotton there, and I was just married; but there was so much discrimination that I just gave up; I just traveled [thru] . . ." (Fabens respondent).

At the beginning of World War II, many local Fabens youth were drafted. The older men who remained in Fabens could, by 1942, earn about $4.50 to $5.50 per day in the cotton fields. But there was more pay and work in road and construction projects, as well as in the defense industries of California (as well as El Paso and Arizona). More Blacks and some working-class Whites appeared in the Fabens work force during this time. Many worked in cotton gin and compress processing. Also, as laborers were brought in large numbers from Mexico to work as farm laborers, overall wage levels fell and increased unemployment among Fabens workers and also motivated other workers to seek work in California.

After the war many of the older men who left for California, and the surviving young men from the military service, returned to Fabens. Nevertheless, the economic prospects for new families were dim. In 1945–1950, the total value of cotton produced yearly in the El Paso Valley jumped by 297%, exports under the Marshall Plan boomed, profits soared, large-scale hiring of braceros on 1-year contracts expanded, and veterans were unable to find jobs with wages, hours, and working conditions to their satisfaction in the Fabens area (Reschenthaler, 1968, pp. 20–21).

Mexican Nationals and Their Effect on Labor in the Fabens Area

The use of Mexican national as workers was controversial and had three important effects in the Fabens area. First, it lowered overall wages in agriculture and in other industries (e.g., construction and mining). Second, it severely reduced the ability of small farmers to compete with larger farmers and drove many off their land. Third, it created an environment where others could not effectively compete in the labor market, and so many moved out of the Fabens area.

The 1942 Agricultural Agreement did not provide provisions for the admission of Mexican nationals to the El Paso workforce, although they were admitted to other border farm areas, "primarily because it was plagued by discrimination, low wages, and lack of personal or job protection" (Reschenthaler, 1968, p. 22). In 1947, Congress replaced the agreement with Public Law 40 which permitted entry of farm workers from Mexico. A new international agreement had not been reached, however, so thousands of workers were crossing the border illegally to work in the United States.

> In 1948, according to estimates at the time, up to ninety percent of the work on the farms of El Paso Valley was done by Mexican nationals. Farm wages were extremely low and continued to decline in the El Paso-Trans-Pecos area. Drives by the American labor unions to organize the farm workers were unsuccessful, since in most instances the laborers were illegally in the country. Native farm labor was driven from the areas where the Mexicans had come to work because the aliens accepted "starvation" wages and the most degrading work conditions. (Reschenthaler, 1968, p. 23)

Thus, when the 1948 harvest came due, there was a severe labor shortage. By October, thousands of workers throughout Mexico had gathered at Juarez; those interviewed said they had been led to expect $3 per hundred pounds (about $6 per day) for picking cotton on American farms in the Valley. But American border officials claimed the agreement which was then being negotiated would be for the "prevailing wage," which they indicated was $2 a hundred in the El Paso area. When Mexican officials refused to open the border, the El Paso district U.S. immigration director had the bridges opened, and claimed that Mexico had broken the agreement. As the workers crossed, the immigration service "arrested" them and "paroled" them to the Texas Employment Commission, which put them to work on local farms (Reschenthaler, 1968).

Wages plummeted and, of course, benefited large farmers.

> Cheap foreign labor is advantageous to the owners of the large-scale farms which employ stoop labor in large quantities. Such farms are only 2 percent of the nation's farm units, approximately 125,000, and only a fraction of this small number employs most of the alien farm workers. This cheap labor is in competition with the great group of family-type farms. (United States, 1951, p. 17)

It is thus highly likely that the use of cheap illegal labor hastened the process by which small farms were bought out and absorbed by larger farms, which could employ large numbers of illegal laborers and effectively use new mechanized methods.

A new U.S.–Mexico agreement was signed in July, 1949, and approved by Congress in 1951, which was intended to protect braceros by providing for contracts of only 3 to 6 months, and proposed a no recruitment right along the border, and would levy fines and forfeiture of a bond for employers who failed to account for workers they had hired.[4] But for the most part these new regulations were ignored and the boom continued (Reschenthaler, 1968).

Mexican nationals with work passes were increasingly being hired in industries outside of agriculture. Their numbers swelled in such industries as construction, services, and other industries.

> As a result, wages were driven down to deprivation levels. Labor conditions were especially bad in some service industries. In hotels and restaurants, for example, Mexicans would work for as little as $2.00 a day, of which they would pay $1.15 to busboys and other employees to insure their jobs for the following day. By the end of 1948, according to a reliable report, aliens who had entered the United States held between 6,000 and 9,000 non-agricultural jobs in El Paso. (Reschenthaler, 1968, p. 25)

So despite the increased standard of living among farmers and businessmen, the working class in Fabens found little incentive to remain in the area, expect for familial and social relations that had been developed over time. There were strong "push" incentives for local residents to pick up and leave for Arizona or California, where the use of Mexican nationals had decreased.

The Emergence of the Middle Class and the Struggle for Power in Fabens

While most young working-class Mexican Americans left Fabens, a few were able to earn a living in Fabens and even realize some upward economic mobility as members of a new middle class. This new group was centered in the Yucca Heights and sections of the Papalote area.

With middle-class Anglos, many of whom were post-war newcomers to Fabens, the new Mexican-American middle class were able to find white-collar employment in new industries and in offices in El Paso, or as white-collar workers in the services associated with a mechanized agricultural industry.

The existence of this middle-class group is significant in terms of Fabens' racial history. It marked the first time that Mexican Americans and Anglos mingled in terms of residence and schooling, leading eventually to primary school desegregation in the 1950s. Pressure for desegregation was brought about by middle-class Mexican Americans and their Anglo allies who did not want their children to face the same educational barriers they had faced as children. This victory by the middle class was important because it challenged a social system that had been in place for years and benefited, for the most part, a small, but powerful, landed gentry. The emergence of the middle class in Fabens was a direct challenge to the power long held by big farming interests.

At this time, there also was an effort to reduce the town's dependence on large farming by introducing other industries. A number of businesses were started. For example, the Fabens Development Corporation was formed with a capital outlay of $60 from 60 men. The money was spent on 35 acres of vacant land northeast of town, near the airport. A small shop, the Border Clothing Factory, began operation on the site but failed, some say because it lacked strong leadership. Attempts to bring a Sears clothing subsidiary, and a "Tex-Togs" plant failed. Some Fabens residents believe it failed because of opposition and lack of full support by big farmers, who feared the introduction of competing, higher paying jobs, the threat of unionization, and the emergence of a strong, competing political and economic group.

The conflict blossomed in 1953 when a group of small businessmen began circulating a petition which, if it received 30 signatures, would authorize a popular referendum on incorporation. Several informants claim that before the signatures could be collected, certain big farmers called the small businessmen among the signers and threatened to withdraw their business from their business establishments if the signatures were not withdrawn. The signatures were withdrawn and the petition campaign scrapped.

Notes

1. There are many examples of these procedures used by Anglos and their allies to oust small farmers from their land. For instance, one informant indicated that J. P. Miller, a big farmer, fenced in 25 acres of land belonging to one of the original Mexican inhabitants and then ran him off. In 1917–1918, Jesus Nunez was driven off his land by a land investment company—"they burned down his buildings, tore down his fences, he died in the county poor house."
2. Wages in 2010 dollars.
3. There are several statistics that highlight the dire situation among farmers during the Great Depression. To begin with, crop and stock prices dropped.

Indeed, cotton dropped to 5.5 cents per pound; corn dropped by 19.4 cents per bushel, and the price of hogs dropped from $7.24 per hog to $2.94 (see Perkins, 1969). Farm foreclosures also increased during this period. In 1926, there were 17.4 farm foreclosures per 100 farms and by 1933 the rate rose to 38.8 farm foreclosures per 100. Indeed, in 1933 over 200,000 farms went into foreclosure (Alston, 1983).

4. It should be noted that during the war years (1940–1945) most of the braceros, or contract laborers from Mexico (63% in 1945) were employed in California. In California, cotton wages went up 136% compared to an increase of 326% in Texas. In the ensuing 4 years, California employed relatively few braceros (8% in 1949), and raised their wages by about 15%. In the meantime, Texas employers hired the major share of braceros (46% in 1949) and were able to lower the cotton wage by 11% (United States, 1951, pp. 56–58).

5

Background Characteristics of the Fabens Population

Fabens is located in El Paso County in West Texas, about 30 miles southeast of urban El Paso. The El Paso Council of Governments defined the "Fabens regional area" as covering approximately 45 square miles between the Rio Grande on the southwest and the interstate freeway (IH10) on the northeast, and between the village of Cuadrilla to the northwest and route FM1190, near the village of Tornillo to the southeast. Nearly all the land between Fabens and the Rio Grande was developed as irrigated farm land, like much of the lower El Paso Valley. Desert lands with gently rolling sand hills and dunes were set between this basically flat area and the interstate freeway. A low escarpment demarcated the irrigated valley land from the desert; a higher escarpment, marking the far edge of the valley, runs, irregularly, parallel to the river's course, usually between 1 and 2 miles northeast of the freeway. The physiography along the river is rocky desert, and mountains lie beyond on both sides.

The Yellow Rose, pages 41–50

Fabens and its regional area share a semi-arid, hot desert climate with El Paso and much of the American Southwest and Chihuahua, Mexico. The average year-round temperature, based on the years 1931 to 1967, is 63.3°F. Humidity is extremely low. Precipitation is mainly in the form of rain from cloudbursts and thunderheads.

Fabens was unattractive. Beyond those few upper- and middle-class homes on the town's north side, there was little grass or greenery to be seen. Houses, for the most part, tended to be constructed of adobe or concrete blocks. Junk-filled vacant lots adjoin the backyards of many lower-class homes. Many stores along Main Street were vacant, with their interiors piled with debris. Building facades on the street were shabby and depressing. The interiors of surviving businesses were dim, dull, and dirty looking.

The town was bounded on three sides by cotton fields. On the north, the desert begins abruptly but inches from the last watered lawn or back fence. The desert area is scrubby and scattered with vegetation. Yet, the Valley in which the town sits presented an interesting rugged view from the highway. Fabens by all appearances was a dying town, holding on by only the slimmest of hopes.

Fabens was about 80% developed; the remaining 20% was vacant desert land. About 5% consisted of residential and commercial acreage, including the small community of Cuadrilla, and the small Fabens airport. In addition to the airport, which mainly served agriculture and small recreational planes, a number of other transportation facilities served Fabens. These include the Southern Pacific Railroad (a major transportation system for the Great Migration of the Black population from the South), which ran between El Paso, Sierra Blanca, and San Antonio; the interstate freeway, to which Fabens is connected by the Fabens–Carlsbad Access Road; U.S. 80, which ran through El Paso, Socorro, Clint, Fabens, Tornillo, and rejoins Ft. Hancock; and the North Loop (FM76), the South Loop (FM258), the Island Road, FM 76, the Island–Guadalupe Road, and FM 1190, which served the farmlands around Fabens. Thus, four separate roads connected Fabens with El Paso, and the trip could be made by auto in under a half hour; it was an even shorter trip on the expressway. The new limited access express route lies less than 2 miles north of Fabens and was reached directly via Fabens Street, a main town artery. A sprawling new shopping center on El Paso's outskirts was a 20 minute drive from Fabens by expressway.

Fabens lies several miles north of the Rio Grande, which, for most of its length along the lower Valley, is but a trickling stream several feet wide and only inches deep. One formal crossing (manned by the Border Patrol and U.S. Customs) lies a few minutes south of town opposite the Mexican town of Caseta. Another crossing lies 20 minutes west of town. Mexico, in short, is next door and easily accessible. Mexican food, night life, TV and radio stations, and ambience were available to any Mexican American and Anglo Fabens resident.

The town of Fabens had all the basic utilities, including piped gas, telephones, electricity, a sewage system, and piped water. As was the case in much of the region, access to well water was an important consideration in any plans for future development.

Most of the retail businesses of Fabens were located on Main Street. Many small grocery stores, cantinas, and other shops were scattered throughout the predominantly Mexican American residential areas. Ellis Chevrolet Company, the Fabens Airport, the Hicks-Ponder Plant, and some gas stations were located along the access road to the interstate freeway, or near the exit. A strip of land along the railroad track, near the downtown commercial area, was occupied, for the most part, by a cotton gin and compress, and several warehouses.

The census completed by the Fabens Study Project (1969) registered a total of 602 families in the urban area. The figure was nearly identical with the 607 families obtained by a door-to-door census conducted by Project Bravo.

Three-quarters of all household heads were identified as Roman Catholics. Of these, 95% (of the 75%) were Mexican American. Another 18%, mostly Anglos, including 9 of the 11 Black and 10 Mexican-American family heads, were members of Baptist or Methodist churches; in a few cases, Christian, Presbyterian, or other Protestant churches were also represented. Finally, about 3% (16 Mexican Americans and 4 Anglo family heads) identified themselves as members of Evangelical Apostolic congregations.

In 1969, the town of Fabens was divided into three areas. In one area of town there was a section called called *La Tortuga* (The Turtle). This section was the major commercial area of Fabens. It had a family density of about 2,600 families per square mile. Data from the Notre Dame Census indicated that 186 families residing in this area were about 95% Mexican American; and about half of them had five or more members in the family. Fifty-seven percent had yearly incomes of less than $3,000 and 19% had yearly incomes between $3,000 and $5,000. Fifty-nine percent of its working family heads were semi-skilled, service, or unskilled workers; another 11% were skilled workers, and 10% were farm laborers. Eighteen percent of all family heads, however, were not in the labor force—probably reflecting the number of retired family heads and female heads who were receiving welfare payments.

La Tortuga was the most socioeconomically depressed of the three areas: Most of the families earning less than $2,000 per year reside in the area.

Crowding and poor housing also characterize La Tortuga. More than a third of its houses had shabby appearances; the interiors in one-fourth were not much better. This, and the fact that many families almost entirely remodel old, run-down homes rather than move into newer homes, suggests a serious shortage of decent housing in Fabens. In any event, the inhabitants appeared to be doing the best they could to keep up structures which, by their external appearance, ought to have been razed and replaced by new, low-cost housing.

Another area in Fabens was mostly industrial and ran along the railroad tracks, and includes a large residential area called *El Papalote* (The Windmill), and a small area in its north corner where most of the Black families live. About 89% of its 242 families were Mexican American; most of the rest were Anglos. With a family density of 865 families per square mile, this area was considerably less populated than La Tortuga. There was also a greater mixture of middle and lower income families—comprised of Anglos, Mexican American, and Blacks. Half of the families consisted of five or more people: Forty-five percent earned less than $3,000 a year, and another 17% earned between $3,000 and $5,000 annually.

The occupational makeup was very similar to that of La Tortuga: 22% were not in the labor force; of those working, 56% were semi-skilled, service, or unskilled workers; 11% were skilled workers; and 11% farm laborers. A similar pattern of housing quality appeared in the condition of furniture, interiors, and exteriors of the homes, while only 30% of the interiors and 31% of the exteriors were rated as *good.* Moreover, only about a third (37%) of the homes' furniture was rated as being in *good condition.*

Northeast of the tracks and southeast of East Second Street, lay a section of Fabens that was much different from the others in the community. This area included the four major school buildings of Fabens; a middle-class postwar development called Yucca Heights, and a mixture of older, predominantly middle- and upper-class homes, including a section sometimes called the Hill with mostly large, expensive upper-class Anglo homes. The area had a density of only 443 families per square mile, far less than either El Papalote or La Tortuga. In addition, only a quarter of the 97 families had five or more people, about half the proportion of large families in the rest of Fabens. About three quarters of the families were Anglo, the rest Mexican American.

There were significant economic and occupation inequalities in Fabens. To begin with, 14% earned less than $3,000 per year, and, in contrast, 68% earned over $5,000 annually. While there were only five families earning $10,000 or more annually, and were 24 families earning this much. In one area of Fabens, approximately half of the families were headed by professionals, proprietors, managers, or farm owners, and another 17% were white-collar sales, clerical, or kindred workers. Only 17% are semi-skilled, service, or unskilled workers and were concentrated in a small, predominantly Mexican American area near the railroad tracks.

The data from the 1969 survey suggest a pattern in which income was concentrated in the hands of a relatively small group of owners, managers, farmers, businessmen, and professionals, most of whom are Anglo. The working class and poor were mostly Mexican American, living in shabby homes with large families.

Population Analysis

During the summer of 1969, a research team from Notre Dame completed census interviews with 602 families in Fabens, Texas. The Notre Dame Census included the entire urbanized area of Fabens, and a sample of farms in the surrounding area. The farm sampling area was much larger than that which was generally thought of as comprising Fabens. But since the farmers in this area are an integral part of life in the Fabens community, it was decided to use this larger area as the base. There were 37 refusals in the urban area, and three refusals in the farming sample. Census results indicated that 105 of these families were owners and 218 were laborers. The sample of 40 families was slightly less than a 10% sample. Thus, the area of Fabens included in this study has a population of some 885 families.

Demography

The 602 families comprised a population of about 2,803 persons, of whom 2,666 were residents of the urbanized Fabens area. Data are displayed in Table 5.1. The census data revealed that Mexican American families averaged

TABLE 5.1 Selected Characteristics of Fabens' Families

Characteristic	Mexican Americans	Anglos	Blacks
Completed	456	135	11
Refusals	20	20	0
Families	456	135	11
Both Spouses Present	343	99	7
Children	1,390	188	33
Other Relatives	116	20	5

Source: Fabens survey by Notre Dame Research Team, 1969

about 5 persons per family, Anglo families about 3 persons per family, and Black families averaged about 5 persons. Given these figures, it seems safe to say that the area of Fabens had a population size somewhere between 2,800 and 4,300 persons.

The majority (75%) of families residing in the urbanized area of Fabens were of Mexican ancestry. On the other hand, the majority of farms were owned by Anglos, while nearly all the farm laborers were Mexican American. Again, about 75% of the farm-related families were Mexican American. (Keep in mind that a small number of farm owners actually resided within the urbanized area of Fabens.)

Table 5.2 displays selected population characteristics of the Fabens population by household and ethnicity. Mexican American families were about 74% of the population, Anglos about 24%, and Blacks 2%. Nearly 75% of both Mexican-American and Anglo families were intact at the time of the census. Upon examining the data a bit closer, it was found that a majority of non-intact Anglo families were made up of older persons living alone, while among Mexican-American families young children with either the mother or father or an older relative were present.

Fertility differs by ethnicity as well. Data in Table 5.2 also shows the number of children under age 21 and over age 21 living at home. Thus, while Mexican-American families averaged just a bit over three children per

TABLE 5.2 Selected Characteristics of the 602 Households by Ethnicity

Trait	Mexican Americans	Anglo	Black	Total
Household	456	135	11	602
Spouse present	343	99	7	449
Children < 21	1,278	174	32	1,484
Children > 21	112	14	1	127
Grandchildren < 21	57	0	1	58
Grandchildren > 21	5	1	9	6
Niece–Nephew	4	0	0	4
Grandparent	2	0	1	3
Son, daughter-in-law	29	12	0	41
Brother, sister-in-law	17	2	0	19
Aunt, Uncle	1	0	0	1
Other relative	0	0	2	2
Other non-relative	1	5	1	7
Total Individuals	**2,306**	**441**	**56**	**2,803**

Source: Survey by Notre Dame Research Team, 1969.

family, Anglo households averaged only 1.4 children per family. These differences remain fairly stable even by restricting the analysis to families with children under 21. In this case, Mexican-American families averaged about 2.8 children and Anglo families about 1.3 children. The small Black population averaged about 3 children per family, indicating that their fertility rate was very close to that of Mexican Americans. Again, data in Table 5.2 show that Mexican-American families were more likely to include other relatives in the household than Anglo families. The percentage differences were 25.5% for Mexican Americans, and only 15% among Anglo families.

In this section, I make the following comparisons:

- Mexican Americans and Anglos
- Age–sex comparisons between Fabens and Texas
- Age–sex comparisons with the United States

Perhaps the most striking result was that well over 54% of the Fabens population were under 19 years of age. This figure was much closer to the population distributions found in developing countries than it was for Texas or for the rest of the United States: 41% in Texas in 1960, and 39% in the United States in 1964.

The group under age 20 was strikingly similar to young adults of Fabens; that is, the group between the ages of 20 and 39. This age cohort was born during the depression and the period just after World War II. While it is to be expected that the cohort born during the depression would be smaller than another age grouping, it is nevertheless somewhat surprising to see that the post-war baby boom group was smaller in Fabens. Such a result tends to verify the commonly held opinion among Fabens leaders that it was losing its young people via out-migration. Moreover, it appears that young men were more likely to leave than young women.

The middle age group, 49 to 59, also was small. This was expected because of the depression and World War II—in both cases, men comprised a smaller percentage of this age cohort. More importantly, the age pyramid reflected sharp differences between Mexican Americans and Anglos. Anglos were clustered more evenly throughout the age distribution, while Mexican Americans were clustered among younger age groups. The implications for the future of the community are extremely important.

While Anglos comprised about one quarter of the families in Fabens, they were only about 16% of the total population. Mexican Americans, on the other hand, comprised about 84% of the census population in the community. If both groups exhibit equal out-migration, the prospects were that Mexican-American families would be an even larger share of the Fabens population.

General Characteristics of Household Heads

Table 5.3 summarizes the major characteristics of household heads in Fabens in 1969. The single largest proportion of household heads were between the ages of 41 to 60. Mexican-American household heads were more likely to be under age 21 than Anglo household heads, but more likely to have household heads under 40–37% versus 30%. At the other extreme, Anglos were more likely than Mexican Americans (33% to 25%) to have household heads age 61 and over.

TABLE 5.3 Major Characteristics of Household Head

	Mexican Americans	Anglo	Black	Total
Age of Household Head by Ethnicity				
< 21	13	2	0	15
22–40	155	38	3	196
41–60	171	53	6	230
61+	115	41	2	158
Unknown	1	2	0	3
Total	**455**	**136**	**11**	**602**
Place of Birth of Household Heads				
Mexico	196	1	0	197
Fabens	115	9	1	125
El Paso	36	15	1	52
Other Texas Area	84	47	4	135
New Mexico	11	8	0	19
U.S. not TX or NM	13	53	5	71
Neither TX or NM	1	2	0	3
Total	**456**	**135**	**11**	**602**
Sex of Household Head				
Male	355	112	6	473
Female	101	23	5	129
Total	**456**	**135**	**11**	**602**
Citizenship and Ethnicity of Household Heads				
U.S.	311	131	11	453
Mexican	145	2	0	2
Neither	0	2	0	2
Total	**456**	**135**	**11**	**602**

(continued)

TABLE 5.3 Major Characteristics of Household Head (continued)

	Mexican Americans	Anglo	Black	Total
Education of Household Head by Ethnicity				
None	109	1	0	110
Elementary	198	20	4	222
8th Grade	40	10	1	51
Some H.S.	49	24	0	73
H.S.	46	30	3	79
Some College	4	19	0	23
College Graduate	3	23	0	26
Work	1	6	0	7
Other	6	2	3	11
Total	**456**	**135**	**11**	**602**
Employment Status of Household Head by Ethnicity				
Full Time	276	99	5	379
Part Time	56	4	2	62
Retired	45	16	1	62
Student	2	0	0	2
Other	2	0	0	2
NILF	75	3	3	94
Total	**456**	**11**	**11**	**602**

Source: Data from the Notre Dame Research Team

Nearly two fifths of Mexican-American household heads were born in Mexico, while the largest percentage of Anglo household heads were born outside of the Southwest (39%). The next largest place of origin among Mexican-American household heads was either Fabens or El Paso, and for Anglos some other area in Texas. Thus, Mexican-American household heads tended to be indigenous to the area—that is, indigenous in the sense of having been born in or around Fabens and the Mexican border area—whereas Anglos were not. It was also found that in 1969 about one quarter of the household heads in Fabens hold Mexican citizenship. As noted earlier, one quarter of the household heads (for both Mexican Americans and Anglos) were either single, separated, divorced, or widowed. For Anglos, widowed was the single largest category, and separated or divorced characterized Mexican-American household heads.

There were significant socioeconomic differences between the ethnic groups. Educationally, 67% of Mexican-American household heads had completed fewer than 8 years of formal schooling compared to 16% among Anglo household heads. Moreover, 37% of Anglos and only 2% of Mexican Americans had any college education whatsoever. What was truly significant, however, was that there was such a small percentage of Mexican-American household heads with a high school diploma. The history of public education in the United States, and Texas in particular, shows that schools have been slow in assisting minorities improve their socioeconomic status (Verdugo, 1986).

The majority of household heads were employed full time. There was a large number who were retired or not in the labor force, but this closely mirrored the number of heads who were over 61 years of age. A significant percentage of Mexican-American household heads were working part time. And, finally, while heads of households were males, a greater proportion of Mexican-American than Anglo household heads were female (22% versus 17%).

Summary

In summary, household heads in Fabens were, for the most part, married, U.S. citizens, received limited education, were born in Fabens or in communities nearby, and were between the ages of 30 and 50. Among Mexican-American household heads, a significant number maintained their Mexican citizenship, spoke little or no English, had little or no formal education, and were employed part time.

As has been the case with other studies of Mexican Americans, Mexican Americans in Fabens were poor, had high fertility rates, and had somewhat stable marriages (Browning & McLemore, 1964). Nevertheless, unlike some other areas, Fabens seemed to be losing adult males to big cities like El Paso rather than keeping them in the community. It is difficult to draw any conclusions from the available data as to what extent the decline in the Fabens's population reflected a national trend that began in the United States between 1910 and 1920—a steady movement from rural to urban areas. In any event, if the Fabens population was to increase in the years ahead it would be its urban, non-farm population that would increase. It was anticipated that as Fabens becomes a part of the El Paso metropolitan area it would begin to attract and retain those individuals who were leaving the community for better job prospects elsewhere.

6

Education and the Schools

An educational system perpetuates stasis and mobility. In terms of race or ethnicity, the role taken by education in its dual functions depends upon the degree of racial stratification prevalent in the community. The greater the rigidity of stratification, the more likely the educational system perpetuates a system of race-based stasis.

The history of education in Fabens suggests that it was and continues to perpetuate racial stratification in the community: Few Mexican Americans received a high school education, and fewer yet attended college. In examining how the educational system in Fabens perpetuates racial stratification several topics are examined:

1. A brief history of education in the community.
2. Trends of educational achievement over time.
3. The views parents, students, and teachers had of one another and of schooling in Fabens.

The Yellow Rose, pages 51–70

A Short History of Fabens' Schools

In 1905, C. F. White and Pat O'Donnell, Sr., decided to start a school because there were 12 children in Fabens who needed an education. They received permission to do so by the county superintendent and a school was opened on the Henry Farm in 1905. John Phalen, an elderly man in his seventies who had moved west because of his wife's health, taught in the one room schoolhouse.

On the night of January 6, 1906, the Fabens' schoolhouse and all its furnishings burned to the ground and Fabens was without a school. In 1909, Charlie Newman donated the first block of land for a school, and was able to collect $500 in cash for the new school. On December 1, 1909 the school was completed. It had one room and was also used on Sunday by the Methodist Church, the minister from Clint held services there once a month. Fifteen children were enrolled in the school.

In 1913, Marciano Rey donated a bell to the school. Josie Silva taught during the school year of 1913–1914 and had eighty students. Many of the children were from families that had left Mexico due to the revolution. The children spoke no English, and despite their age range (from 7 to 14 years of age) they were placed in the first grade. In later years, the school building was abandoned and later purchased by J. M. Escajeda who turned the building into an apartment house.

As Fabens continued to grow, students were educated in a two-room building. The next school was held in a huge tent. The land for the tent school would eventually become the site of the Baptist Church.

In 1917, the Cobos School was completed at a cost of $10,000. It was named after Jesus Cobos, an original school board member. Lorenzo Madrid was in charge of construction, with Federico Aguilar as his assistant. In 1918 and 1919, the Cobos School was turned into a hospital. Dr. F. D. Cooke, an army surgeon, along with three orderlies, were in charge. The first sign of stratification in the school system occurred in 1925 when the Cobos School became the Latin-American School, and Anglo students were transferred to the new grammar school. The one-room high school in Bungalow Courts was moved to the upstairs part of the grammar school. The Cobos School was torn down in 1948, and became the site for Fabens High School.

Miss Myra Winkler, the county superintendent from 1912 to 1924, suggested that one large high school in Fabens could serve both Fabens and Tornillo and would be a logical solution because neither town had enough students to justify one high school. Tornillo inhabitants opposed the plan and eventually withdrew from the district. The division of the Fabens

School District into the Fabens and Tornillo districts was formally approved on February 11, 1923.

La Isla School was situated in the home of the Sierra family in the early part of the 20th century. John Phelan and Ashley Gillet were taught in the school. In 1914, Miss Ellen Kelly, who boarded in the Sierra household, opened a school in the Federico Arroyo store. In 1914, the new school was built on the Island just northwest of the Catholic church. The school was turned into a hospital during the 1918 and 1919 influenza epidemic. About 1926, the island consolidated the Fabens School District. In 1928, the island school was closed.

The grammar school, built in 1924, served as both a grammar school and as a high school until about 1948 or 1949.

The first Black school in Fabens, the Carver School, was constructed from railroad ties and was located between Tornillo and the Hudspeth county line. Mrs. M. A. Bates taught the 13 students that attended in 1924. In the spring of 1939, a two-room apartment was rented about two blocks east of the Carver School, and a Mrs. Ceristella Priestly, a substitute teacher from El Paso, commuted back and forth to provide instruction. Mrs. Priestly did not have a degree, and members of the Black community requested a more qualified teacher.

In 1949, Fabens built a new depot and the old building was moved behind the Camp School and was used as the school for Black students. The building was abandoned in 1951. During the school year of 1949–1950, the board of education received numerous complaints about the condition of the building. The board investigated and took action. The one-room building was erected in 1951, and was built at a cost of $2,800.

The first high school in Fabens was a one room in the Bungalow Courts. In 1925, the high school was moved to the upstairs classrooms of the new grammar school building. In the Spring of 1926, three students graduated from high school. Lobbying for a new high school in Fabens began in 1940. The school board had decided that it was inappropriate to have high school and grammar school students in the same building. The high school was completed in 1950 at a cost of about $288,000.

The School Plant in 1969: A General Description

In 1969, the Fabens Independent District served approximately 70 square miles of El Paso County. The district operated a 12-grade program for 1,550 students, of which 80% were Mexican American, 19% Anglo, and 1% Black.

The district operated four separate campuses. All school campuses were located within the urbanized Fabens area.

Revenue sources for the 1969–1970 academic year were:

State	$530,554
Local	$192,271
Federal	$58,247
Transfers	$600

Federal sources (about 7% of the total revenue) were mainly used for the Head Start project through Project Bravo but it was operated by the school system. The program operated during the academic year 1968–1969, and accepted students under the age of 5 who belonged to families with incomes of $3,500 or less.

The Adult Education Program served people 18 or older who had not completed elementary school. Judging from the number of people who attended (200), the program was extremely successful. But when Project Bravo initiated a similar program and also offered to pay students, the school program was displaced. The primary emphasis of the Project Bravo program was teaching English.

The Fabens School District employed a professional staff of 78. The staff included the superintendent, full-time principals for each campus, librarians, a counselor, and 69 teachers: 20 in the high school, 21 in the grade school,13 in O'Donnell, and 15 in the primary school. According to the report from the Texas Education Agency the staff additionally included, a social worker, a nurse, and three teacher's aides.

A 1969 report by the Texas Education Agency indicated that while facilities seemed adequate there were some updates needed, such as more classrooms, better lighting, and showering facilities for the high school (Texas Education Agency 1969.

The school board functioned as a body of policy making and appraisal. The superintendent was considered the chief executive officer and in charge of administering the district's education program. School personnel were employed upon recommendation by the superintendent and were assigned to positions by the board.

The Board of Education held public meetings every month, and public records were archived. The administrative policies by which the district was governed were published and made available to interested parties.

The state required that textbooks be changed every 5 years. A state textbook committee formed by superintendents, examined, revised, and presented its views to schools within the state, along with several options for each subject. The local textbook committee, formed by teachers, decided which option to pursue.

The high school program for the 1969–1970 academic year offered a variety of elective and required courses. Vocational courses consisted of those in homemaking and agriculture.

There were two tracks in the high school: a general one for students not planning to attend college, and a college preparatory track. Students had the option of changing from general to college prep as late as their junior year.

Two members of the Notre Dame Research Team visited the high school counselor's office and examined student test files. The inspection revealed that there was no systematic record keeping. Instead, information on the IOWA, ASUAB, and other tests were found for some students and not others. Detailed scores were found on the IQ Gamma Form, but again for only some students.

The most recent scores that could be found in the files were dated October 1968, others September 1966. Some test scores found in the files were not dated at all. Other important data, such as age and class group to which the students belonged, could not be determined. To say the least, the condition, comprehensiveness, and utility of the testing materials left much to be desired. There were a total of 184 test scores and had the following distribution (see Table 6.1).

The Fabens School Teacher

In an effort to obtain some information about Fabens school teachers, questionnaires were sent to all teachers in the Fabens school district. Twenty-three answered (31% response rate), and the following data were computed (see Table 6.2).

TABLE 6.1 Student Test Scores

119 and above	2
110–119	7
90–109	53
80–89	62
70–79	56
70 and below	4
Total	**184**

TABLE 6.2 Selected Characteristics of Fabens School Teachers

Age	Percent	Years Taught, General	Percent
22–27	26	1–3	35
31–35	17	4–6	17
44–48	22	10–15	13
50–58	17	20–25	26
60–65	17	30–40	9
Credentials		**Years Taught, Fabens**	
BA	66	1–3	47
Working on MA	13	4–6	13
MA	17	7–10	13
No Answer	4	11–15	9
		16–20	9
		20–25	9
Teaching Certificate		**Residence During the Year**	
Permanent	83	Fabens	78
Temporary	13	El Paso or near Fabens	22
None	4		
Present Address			
Fabens	65		
El Paso or near Fabens	17		
Texas	0		
Our of Texas	8		

Source: Notre Dame Research Team, 1969.

Teachers' Views and Opinions on Materials and Resources

The allocation of resources is a central component in achieving objectives. For schools, tax revenues comprise important resources that are used to pay salaries and cover the costs of the schools' physical facilities. Given the importance of resources, teachers were asked the following question about the allocation of school funds: "How is the budget determined?" Surprisingly, 60% did not know. One stated: "I did not know there is any." Thirty-nine percent felt that it was adequate for the teaching needs they had. Thirty-four percent thought it was not adequate. Teachers were also asked to describe the materials used in their classes. When asked if materials were sufficient and adequate, 56% answered yes; 28% said no. One said, "One can always add to what is in use." Of the ones that responded "No," some also indicated that they personally had purchased their own materials.

What about school facilities that should be provided by the school? Thirty-nine percent of teachers mentioned improving materials such as film strips, books, slides, Spanish literature, bilingual stories; 13% wanted smaller classes, and 15% felt that nothing needed improvement.

Selecting textbooks is an issue related to materials and resources. Teachers were asked to identify textbooks they were using and to give their opinion about the appropriateness of these textbooks for the level of students they taught. A majority (52.5%) said the books were appropriate; some added "very modern and up-to-date." Thirty percent felt their appropriateness was limited, and 9% felt that they were of no use at all.

Teachers were asked: "How much influence do you have in the selection of textbooks for your class?" Fifty-two percent felt that they could effectively select and recommend books. Eighteen percent thought they had no influence whatsoever, and 14% felt that their opinions were not weighed enough or that they had very little influence on the final decision. Nine percent did not have the slightest idea if they could or could not influence the selection of their textbooks.

So then, how are the textbooks selected? Eighty-two percent of the teachers said that teachers' committees or panels select texts from the samples sent to the school by the state book committee. Some added that the administration participated in these committees. Eighteen percent thought the administration ignored the way the school selected the textbooks.

Teachers Evaluate the School System

Sixty percent of the teachers liked, preferred, and planned to stay in the Fabens school system. When asked why, 57% replied that it was because of the good climate, because a big city was nearby, or because they had families in the area. Some felt that school conditions were terrific: "the administration is cooperative, not pushy or nosy," "it is a progressive growing system," "ideal working conditions. . . ." One teacher replied, "Climate nice, no night meetings, but if they do not give me better pupils I may resign."

Teachers also were asked to evaluate the school system's strongest and weakest points. Thirty-four percent felt the school system's strongest point was the personal contact teachers had with students something which helped to improve both the community and the youth of Fabens. Twelve percent identified the school system's strongest point as the freedom teachers had; that is, no interference by the principal or superintendent. Twelve percent mentioned excellent teaching colleagues, an excellent administration, and a good overall operation. Eight percent felt there were no strong points.

Though teachers had complaints about the school system, their complaints appeared to be somewhat random: 12% felt that teachers were prejudiced against Mexican Americans, another 12% said that the curriculum should be revised to meet the needs of a diverse studentry. Some felt that programs to prepare students effectively for college or jobs should be sought. One fourth felt that the school's weakness was an external one, the community or parents, and a lack of cooperation or help. Other teachers' complaints were: "Low salaries, for this the good teachers leave"; "Money is misused—the tennis court is used just by very few students, better to have used that money for encyclopedias . . . the ones in my room are from 1939!"; "Some teachers are not fully certified."

Parent–Teacher Communication

Parental involvement is important. Teachers know that they can be most effective in helping children if they have the help of parents. One objective of this research was to examine the extent to which parents and teachers cooperated and communicated with one another. The approach taken was to examine how teachers viewed the attitudes, participation, and interest parents had about the education of their children. An additional interest was in determining whether parents felt teachers had an interest in their children. Teachers and parents disagreed considerably on these issues, and teachers were more likely to have had the more intense feelings.

Teachers were asked what they believed were the attitudes of parents toward education. The majority of teachers felt that parental attitudes varied by parental groups. Fifty-six percent of teachers felt that parents did not care at all about their children's education, and that parent's cultural back [being Mexican American] parents did not expect their children to attend college. "They see education as a necessary evil," one teacher commented.

By contrast, some teachers felt that Anglo parents wanted a college education for their children and as some teachers suggested, "They have the money for it." A group of teachers suggested that a program through the school could help change the attitudes of Mexican-American parents so that they might encourage their children to pursue a college education. Parents had a different view. Fully 85% of parents claimed to have spoken to their children about the possibilities and advantages of going to college. In addition, 88% of Mexican-American students (and 95% of Anglo students) felt that their parents were "strongly for" education. What they need, a teacher said, referring to the students, is "confidence in themselves." This particular teacher continued by saying that confidence about attending college does not have its origins in the family; rather, it is the teacher who must develop student confidence.

When teachers were asked with which group of parents they best communicated, the answers reflected language differences between parents and teachers. Some teachers insisted that they get along well with "any parent who can speak English." Others said they got along well with those parents who were interested in the education of their children. Thirty percent said they could communicate with every parent and also said they know most of the parents by visiting the students' homes.

Nevertheless, "What about the level and desirability of parental participation in school matters?" Teachers responded (82%) that parents hardly ever or only occasionally took an active interest in such matters. But nearly all (96%) of teachers felt that the parents' participation in school matters, would be desirable, and generally helpful. Teachers (69%) wanted to see parents interested in the policies of the school, in the problems that their children had, and be willing to discuss these problems with teachers. Some teachers suggested that what was needed most was a sense of confidence by both sides. "They [the parents] ought to have enough confidence to come to speak [to us]."

Parents expressed much satisfaction with the school system. Eighty-two percent felt that teachers were very interested in their children. Eighty-six percent were satisfied with the education that their children were receiving. Ninety-four percent thought that parent–teacher communication was desirable and generally helpful, even though only 48% had occasionally met the teachers of their children, and 46% admitted that they did not know their children's teachers. Of the 43% who had participated in school matters, the majority had limited their activity to school social events or voting for members of the board of education.

Parents were asked how they viewed and how they would like to see their participation in the school. Forty-eight percent thought they, in cooperation with teachers, should be interested in their children's problems. Other

TABLE 6.3 Parents and Teacher's Opinions of Education

	Percent
Teachers who answered that parents were not interested in education	56
Parents satisfied with the education of children	86
Parents happy about the interest of teachers	82
Parents felt their opinions were respected	61

Source: Notre Dame Research Team.

parents either did not know what their participation in school should be or they thought there was little for them to do. A very typical comment was "parents just have unhappy experiences with the school." A majority of parents (61%) felt that their opinions were respected by the school. This must be contrasted with the fact that only 39% of teachers felt their opinions were respected by the parents of their students. Teachers put the blame on the students: "Students destroy teachers' opinions of parents..."

Parents believed the education their children were receiving was excellent compared to the education they had received themselves. The majority were satisfied with the educational system because they compared it with their own educational experiences, which were not positive.

Parents' and Teachers' Views About Teachers

Student self-esteem is a sensitive topic. One factor that may affect students' self-esteem is the disparity between their social background and that of their teachers. Another factor may be socioeconomic differentials between students themselves.

In Fabens, the majority of pupils came from working class and poor Mexican-American families. Students found themselves being taught by Anglo teachers (only three of the 69 teachers on the Fabens staff in 1969 were of Mexican-American descent), where Anglo children were predominantly middle class, with worldviews close to those of teachers. In this section we examine the perceptions parents and teachers had of the Fabens school teacher.

Twenty-six percent of the teachers felt that if more Mexican-American teachers were hired, it would enhance the relations between parents and teachers. Furthermore, teachers felt that the presence of Mexican-American teachers would increase student–teacher relations, and thus students would talk more freely about their problems. One teacher responded, "Maybe it will help to counteract the idea that the school is a purely Anglo institution." Another teacher saw that it was absolutely urgent to hire more Mexican-American teachers: "Is that not rather obvious?"

One third of the teachers felt that race did not make a difference in the hiring of teachers; instead, the emphasis should be on quality. Two teachers even pointed out that they had seen Anglo teachers more interested in Mexican-American students than Mexican-American teachers.

Fifty percent of parents felt that the faculty was appropriate for a school which was located in a community of different languages and ethnic groups. Nineteen percent did not think the faculty was appropriate and the remainder did not know. When asked to explain their responses, those saying that teachers were appropriate for Fabens replied it was because teachers were familiar with the community, worked hard, and maintained positive relationships with people in the community. The 19% who felt that more Mexican-American teachers should be hired felt such action would improve communication, alleviate discrimination, and help teachers better understand the Mexican-American population.

Parents' and Teachers' Views About the Youth of Fabens

In seeking to understand how teachers perceived their relationship with the youth of Fabens, they were asked: "What do you feel is your principal contribution to the youth of Fabens?" Thirty-four percent said listening and understanding. Thirty percent saw their function as encouraging students to go on to college, to value education and how education would improve their lives. Nine percent felt they could motivate students and enhance their aspirations. The remainder saw their contribution primarily in teaching their specific field or subject matter.

Teachers also were asked if, as part of their activity, they should discuss the importance of education with their students or if this was a topic that should be left to the counselor. Seventy-eight percent felt that teachers should raise it with their students. Some teacher respondents suggested that teachers should be encouraged to discuss this matter with their students. One teacher thought teachers should help students become aware of new possibilities and motivate them to attend college. One teachers commented that, "not many are suited for college."

When teachers were asked, "Do you think your students find school interesting?" Forty-eight percent answered yes. Some felt this was due to "teacher friendliness," another said, "It is because the school situation is better than the home." Thirty-nine percent answered that students were interested to a certain extent.

Some teachers felt that certain "classes are too boring and too many restrictions are put on the students." Thirteen percent said that students were not interested because "they do not care about education." Another commented, "When you are hungry, who cares about reading geography?"

Teachers (78%) recognized that it was harder for some groups of students to get ahead in school. Sixty-five percent thought the cause was cultural, economic, linguistic, and family background. A considerable amount of emphasis was placed on language and on the family. For example, one teacher commented, "If the parents do not care the child does not have paper, pencil…" or "supposedly they [the students' parents] learned English. But they won't speak it. They teach their children Spanish and ridicule English." Some teachers suggested that what all the students need is a "better understanding of their background."

> Parents (42%) also acknowledged that it was harder for some groups to get through school. Eighty-five percent of this group felt that Mexican-American students from poor backgrounds had to work harder; 45% felt there was discrimination against Mexican Americans that resulted in less attention and less effort by teachers; 27% blamed the family: "Parents don't prepare their children for school, they don't teach them English or help them with the homework and dress them properly."

It should be emphasized, however, that this group of parents constituted only 42% of the parent sample. Fully 44% of parents interviewed felt that no group had a particularly hard time in school.

Students' Views of the School

Students were asked several questions about schooling.

Seventy-eight percent of the Anglo and 80% of the Mexican-American students thought that school was interesting. Students were then asked, "What do you like best about school?" Twenty-four percent of Anglos and 21% of Mexican Americans mentioned learning in general and the opportunity to know new things. A sample of student responses were: "I like school when I am presented or shown a way I can really learn something. I like the people." Another student said, "Expressing opinions." Another student said, "That you have the chance to get ahead."

School can also be a place where friendships are developed. Indeed, 18% of Anglo and 30% of Mexican-American students said what they liked best in school was friendship. A sampling of students' responses were: "Students, knowing and learning about them," "the friendships and experiences it brings," "having fun with the group and learning new things."

When asked what they most disliked about the school, 22% of Anglos and 18% of the Mexican Americans mentioned teachers' attitudes, and 19% of the Anglos and 15% of Mexican Americans pointed to teachers' methods of teaching. An Anglo student said: "Being treated like a first grader and being made to go slower than your potential rate of learning." Another student said, "teachers' ways of teaching."

Nineteen percent of the Anglos and 27% of Mexican Americans complained about exams, subjects they have to take, homework, and grades. A few students complained about some of their classmates saying: "I dislike many of the students who think they can run the school."

In an effort to examine differential treatment in the school, students were asked, "Are the teachers fair to all the students or do they tend to favor certain groups?" Sixty-three percent of the Anglos and 52% of the Mexican Americans said that the teachers tended to favor certain groups. Of those students saying teachers tended to favor certain groups, 7% of the Anglos and 53% of the Mexican Americans said they favored Anglo students and 57% of the Anglos and 24% of the Mexican Americans pointed out that the teachers favored those students who are good, smart, attentive, and obedient. Clearly, there are different views among students regarding differential treatment.

Generally, students who said that teachers tend to favor certain groups agreed that it was by "making it easier for them," giving them more privileges and attention. Differences between Anglo and Mexican-American students' views of how favoritism was expressed is a significant finding. Few Anglo students saw teachers as favoring them over Mexican Americans. Over half of the Mexican-American students who observed favoritism in the school, expressed it in terms of ethnicity. Still, it must be noted that only one fourth of the Mexican-American students complained about favoritism based upon ethnicity.

As a consequence, when they were asked whether or not "it was easier for any particular group or groups to get ahead in school," those who said yes (35%) commented again that it was easier for the good students and for Anglo students.

Parental Involvement

An important question about parental involvement in the education of their children is whether it has an important effect on student achievement. Consequently, in order to flesh this question out a bit more, students were asked, "Do you think that parents' participation in school matters is necessary, unnecessary, desirable but not necessary, or neither desirable nor necessary?" Eighty-six percent of Mexican Americans and 59% of Anglos said it was necessary. As to the form of parent involvement in "school matters," 19% of the Anglos and 25% of the Mexican Americans felt that parents should give their opinions about teachers, materials taught, and the administration.

Other students felt that parents should be interested in students' problems and in helping resolve these problems. Sixty-one percent of the students agreed that parent–teacher relationships were valuable. When asked to be more specific, students explained that teachers could become familiar with the background of their students. Such knowledge would assist teachers in helping students resolve problems they might be facing. Some of their responses were: "Teachers will be able to help students with things they do not understand"; "Get an idea of home background." Another student said, "The teachers will understand the students and the parents will understand teachers' positions."

How Are Students Viewed?: Self Views, Views by Parents, and Teachers Views

A considerable body of research has pointed out that teachers' attitudes toward students affects their academic achievement (see Rosenthal & Jacobson, 1968). Similarly, student achievement norms and other attitudes also affect academic achievement. In attempting to understand the normative structure surrounding students, parents, students, and teachers were asked to express their views about students in Fabens.

Generally, teachers in Fabens did not feel students would achieve much after leaving school. Teachers were asked: "Where do you think most of the male students will eventually wind up?" Eighty-two percent felt that male students would end up working in factories, in semi-skilled or skilled jobs; some suggested clerical jobs. Only 10% mentioned, as a last choice, that perhaps a few would achieve professional jobs or go on to college.

When the same question was asked about female students, 61% of teachers responded that they would marry. Some teacher respondents specified, "... and they will raise a large family." A minority (14%) felt the girls would end up in factories or clerical jobs. Only one teacher suggested that perhaps a few would attain a professional occupation.

One teacher commented that there was progress and that it could be seen by the kinds of jobs students were entering. "Before, boys used to work on farms. Now, very few do. Most work at factories and in clerical jobs"; about the girls, the answer was: "Before, they got married or worked as maids; now they are working in factories and offices."

Teachers were also asked to estimate what percentages of boys and girls they felt would continue on to college. The estimates for both girls and boys ranged from 2% to 30%. The average estimated percent for boys was 16%, and 12% for girls.

Parents were asked four questions about their offspring. These data are presented in Table 6.4.

TABLE 6.4 Parents' Views About What Students Will be Doing After Their Schooling

	Anglo	Mexican-American
Work Most Probably Be Doing:		
Professional work requiting college education	ND	18
Secretarial work/office work	ND	30
Nurse or teacher	ND	7
Anything they like	85	21
Something that will enable them to make a living	ND	7
Don't know	15	5
No response	ND	12
Work Will be Able to Do After Schooling:		
A profession requiring a college education	86	36
Skilled work	ND	2
Anything they want	14	9
Don't know	ND	45
No response	ND	8
Work That Would Like to Do When Finished Schooling?		
Engineer	ND	15
Secretarial/office work	ND	20
Semi-skilled work	ND	2
No Answer	25	6
Prevent From Doing Work?		
Nothing	63	30
Financial problems	ND	47
Don't know*	37	23

Note: ND = No Data

Results suggest that Anglo parents not only had higher expectations for their children, but were clear about their expectations. Thus, 85% of Anglo parents felt their children could do "anything they like." In contrast, only 21% of Mexican-American parents responded in this way.

When asked what they felt their children would be able to do or like to do, a greater proportion of Anglo parents than Mexican-American parents mentioned professional occupations. Finally, when asked what might prevent their children from doing what they would like to do, 63% of Anglo parents and 30% of Mexican-American parents said: "Nothing would prevent them."

Students were also asked several questions about their own aspirations and views. Results suggested that students, especially Anglo students, had different views about what it was they would do after their education. There were also differences between Anglo and Mexican-American students in their aspirations. What was surprising was the differences between Anglo parents and their children; whereas Mexican-American parents and their children seemed to have similar views. Thus, while 85% of Anglo parents said their children can do "anything they like," only 19% of Anglo students said their parents would like them to do what satisfies them. In contrast, 21% of Mexican-American parents said their children could do anything they like, and 23% of Mexican-American students felt their parents wanted them to do anything that satisfies them.

When asked what kind of work they would like to do after high school, students provided responses dealing more with education than with work. Thus 45% of Anglo and 37% of Mexican-American students said they would go to college; 23% of Anglo and 11% of Mexican-American students mentioned vocational school. So a large percentage of both Mexican American and Anglo youth aspired to continue their education in one form or another.

When asked what they thought would prevent them from achieving their occupational goals, Mexican-American students continued to have views closer to their parents than did Anglo students. Thus, 38% of Mexican-American students felt that financial problems would prevent them from achieving their goals, compared to 30% of their parents who had also mentioned this as a barrier. Among Anglo students, 13% mentioned money or financial barriers, whereas this was not even mentioned by their parents. In fact, among Anglo students 27% felt that nothing would prevent them from achieving their goals whereas 63% of their parents responded in a similar fashion.

Interestingly, 31% of Anglo students and only 8% of Mexican-American students felt that their grades would prevent them from achieving their goals.

Opinions Given by Parents, Students, and Teachers on the Educational Values Transmitted by the School and the Most Important Characteristics of Student Character

As a social institution, the educational system is given the function of not only training youth, but of passing on a society's culture and traditions. These functions can of course be rather broad, and in order to determine

TABLE 6.5 A Comparison of the Coleman Study With Fabens' Youth

	Coleman	Fabens
Parents Disapproval		
Boys	54	46
Girls	53	64
Teachers' Disapproval		
Boys	4	7
Girls	3	4
Breaking With Friends		
Boys	43	46
Girls	43	31

Source: Notre Dame Research Team.

what parents, students, and teachers felt were the values and norms being transmitted in the school, they were asked to select and rank in order of importance those elements they felt to be the most important (see Table 6.5.)

Parents tended to select items emphasizing citizenship and training for work. Thus, as a first choice, 30% of parents selected: "To develop the students' sense of responsibility as a citizen." Thirty-two percent selected: "Prepare students for the work that will give him better living conditions," as a second choice. And, finally, 35% responded: "Prepare the student for an occupation," as a third choice.

Among students, the ordering was slightly different. As a first choice, 23% said, "Prepare the student for the work that will give them better living conditions"; and "Teach the student to read and write." As a second choice, students selected (21%): "Prepare the student for the work that will give them better living conditions"; and "Develop the student's sense of responsibility as a citizen."

The first choice among teachers (26%) was: "Forming students' character." "Developing a sense of responsibility as a citizen," was a second choice (21%). And the third choice among teachers (34%) was: "Prepare students for work leading to decent life."

When asked if Fabens High School transmits the items selected, 48% of teachers said "Yes," while only 28% of students replied similarly. Sixty-two percent of the parents agreed that the Fabens school system transmits the values they had selected.

Student Character Traits

In order to find out more about students' character and the educational system, several questions from the Coleman (1962) study were used. Students were presented with fifteen "characteristics" and asked to select, in order of preference, the five they would most like to have as part of their own character; the same characteristics were presented to teachers and parents.

Anglo parents focused strongly on 4 of the 15 traits. These were creativity, intelligence, truthfulness, and responsibility. The responses of Mexican-American parents, on the other hand, tended to be evenly distributed among the 15 traits with some leaning toward intelligence, practicality, and truthfulness.

As was the case with their parents, Mexican American and Anglo students tended to select different traits. Nevertheless, both Mexican American and Anglo students exhibited more diffused views about character traits. Indeed, students failed to give a majority support to more than one characteristic.

The traits selected by teachers suggested students who fit middle class imagery. Such students were responsible, truthful, cooperative—the kind of student who gives teachers the least trouble, does his work, and allows for nonthreatening creativity.

Differences between Mexican American and Anglo students were interesting. Mexican-American students expressed a desire for more self-confidence. Anglo students were interested in being sociable.

The most important findings may well have been the sharp differences between the viewpoints of teachers and Mexican-American parents, and between Anglos and their children compared to Mexican-American youth and their parents. These findings support the later notion expressed by some scholars that Mexican-American youth are on a path toward assimilation (Alvarez, 1973; Portes & Rumbaut, 2001).

Attitudes and Values

In a rapidly changing, highly rationalized society, the education that the family once provided is taken over by the educational system. Consequently, because children in a community are subjected to the same socialization process, there is a standardization of education, norms, values, and so forth. Moreover, in most cases, because society is constantly changing, youth are exposed to a culture with norms and values different from that of their parents. Coleman (1962) attempted to tap into this divergence between parents and their children.

One question Coleman asked was: "Which would be hardest for you to take: your parents' disapproval, your teachers' disapproval, or breaking with your friends?" Fabens students were asked the same question. Data comparing the responses from Coleman's survey and the responses from Fabens' students are presented in Table 6.5.

The responses from boys in Coleman's sample and those in Fabens' sample indicate that they gave roughly equal weight to the approval of parents and friends. Girls, however, weighed parents' approval more heavily than did boys. This greater need for parental approval among girls was all the more striking among Fabens girls than among girls in the entire United States. The suggestion was that traditional values in small rural communities were quite strong. Though teacher's approval was not generally desired, Fabens students gave greater weight to their teacher's approval than did respondents in Coleman's study.

When these data are stratified by ethnicity, it appears that Mexican-American students are more interested in the approval of their parents than are Anglo students. And, on the other hand, Anglo students, quite surprisingly, were more likely to seek the approval of their friends.

Students were then asked, "If you could be remembered for any of the three things below, which one would you want to be: brilliant student, athletic star (boys), leader in activities (girls), or most popular?" The results from this question was quite similar to those obtained by Coleman (see Table 6.6).

Coleman gave students a series of sentence completion questions: "More than anything, I would like to . . ."; "The best thing that could happen to me this year at school would be . . ."; "The most important thing in life is . . ."; and "I worry most about. . . ." In Coleman's study there were important sex differences in responses. Girls gave far more importance to being popular and with social relations than did boys.

TABLE 6.6 Evaluating Boys and Girls on Selected Topics

	Boys	Girls
Brilliant Student	28	34
Athletic Star (boys)	42	NA
Leader in Activities (girls)	NA	40
Most Popular	31	20

Source: Notre Dame Research Team

Fabens' students answered somewhat differently. To the question, "More than anything else I would like to . . ."; 19% of the boys and 18% of the girls gave responses reflecting their desire to be popular among their classmates. On the other hand, 22% of the girls and 21% of the boys provided responses expressing academic and occupational achievement. A sample of responses were: "raise my grades," "to make the honor roll," "to get a scholarship that will pay all of my expenses to the college of my choice and be accepted by that college." It would appear, then, that Fabens youth seemed more concerned with achievement than with being popular. This was strengthened by their responses to the sentence, "The best thing that could happen to me this year at school would be . . ."; 43% of the boys and 41% of the girls said academic achievement and only 14% of the boys and 17% of the girls provided responses dealing with popularity.

To the sentence, "The most important thing in life . . ."; 30% of the students said being happy and successful. And, finally, to "I worry most about . . ."; 20% of the girls and 14% of the boys responded, "the future"; 17% of the girls and 10% of the boys said "my family"; and an equal percentage of boys and girls (13%) said "grades."

7

Business and the Consumer

As the center of a farming-rural area including both the United States and Mexican sides of the Rio Grande, Fabens had retail and other services that were unusual for a rural town of its size. Indeed, the number of extant businesses was considerably less than that which once flourished during the peak post-war cotton and bracero eras.

In 1969 there were 113 businesses and services plus 9 public utilities, municipal or U.S. services, leading to a total of 122 active businesses or service entities, each with its own office, address, management, and staff. Of the 122 active entities, about 43% were either owned or managed by Mexican Americans.

Selected Characteristics of Fabens' Businesses

Of the total businesses, 32 were surveyed and their manager or owners interviewed. The sample included most of Fabens' larger operations, its food shops, a beauty parlor, and other representatives of small businesses.

The Yellow Rose, pages 71–77

Length of Time in Business

Businesses had been operating in Fabens for some time. Fully 37% had operated for 20 years or more, and 62% had been operating for 11 or more years. With respect to length of time, one prominent businessman noted, "The older, established businesses are essentially paid for by now and most of their owners have reduced their home and other payments substantially, if not completely." The meaning of the respondent's comments are clear—older, established owners were able to continue in their businesses with less profit than would be required by a new business. The respondent continued, "A new business can't come in here and expect to make a living for its owner under present conditions."

Financing a new business was an issue. The president of the Fabens bank felt that under present conditions new businesses could not obtain financing for operating in Fabens even if new jobs were to open in the community. On a personal note, Palemon Fierro, owner of the Boston Store recalled that

> when I first came here, about 40 years ago, I had a small shop and about $4,000 in stock. There were ten other general stores here too. Nevertheless, the streets were so jammed you couldn't move. You'd have a sale and you'd have to shut the doors and let the shoppers in small bunches or you couldn't move in here. The best year I ever had was in '47. Why one day we grossed about $10,000!"

Today, hours can pass without a customer entering the Boston Store.

Within the 4 years prior to 1969, eight businesses had opened in Fabens while 13 had closed their doors. It should be noted that the businesses opened were generally run by local people who were already successfully running another business in town.

Number of Full-Time Employees per Business

There were a surprisingly small number of "one-man operations" in Fabens. The largest nonfarm employer was the Compress with 25 full-time employees. The Compress would take on another 25 workers or so for a 3 to 4 month period annually. There wasn't a company in Fabens that employed as many as the larger farms.

Employment opportunities in Fabens were scarce. The bank president noted that most businesses in town were by now well "shaken down" and operated with the absolute minimum of personnel. Most businesses, he felt, could do substantially more trade without having to increase their staffs.

A bank, for example, needs a teller and certain other positions just to be a bank, regardless of the amount of business or lack of it. So, up to a certain point, few personnel were required.

Starting Salaries Offered

As expected, larger employers started their new employees at or near the state minimum wage. Table 7.1 presents the starting salaries as expressed by 21 businessmen.

Increases in wages were low and ranged from 10 to 15% annually. One large employer, for instance, gave a $.15 cent an hour increase annually. At this rate, a 10 year employee still made $120 or less per month. Raises for unskilled or non white-collar employees were few and low, certainly lower than those of white-collar workers. Town wages were generally higher than farm wages: farm wages ranged from $.75 cents to $1.25 per hour, depending upon illegal labor or length of time employed. Farm foremen rarely earned over $90 per week, though housing and transportation were provided.

Most of the larger town employers provided workers with 50/50 insurance coverage and workmen's compensation programs. Paid vacations were available to some employees.

Percent of Credit Business

Most businesses in Fabens provided some kind of credit to their customers. Table 7.2 provides descriptive data on the amount of credit per total business.

Of those businesses providing credit, 75% or more of the time tended to be large organizations doing business with large farms. Businesses serving the public, were less likely to extend less credit, especially to smaller, mid-sized

TABLE 7.1 Wages in Fabens

Starting Hourly Wage	Businessmen
$0.90	3
1.00	2
1.25	1
1.40	1
1.60	13
1.70	1

Source: Notre Dame Research Team.

TABLE 7.2 Amount of Credit Given by Businesses in Fabens

% of Total Business on Credit	% of Businesses
No credit	18
Less than 10% of sales	7
11 to 25%	10
26 to 50%	10
51 to 75%	13
76 to 100%	42

Source: Notre Dame Research Team.

businesses. Only about a third of pharmacy sales were on credit, for example, while the most successful and largest grocery store did almost three quarters of its business on credit. Observations suggested that smaller shops did substantial business by offering credit, especially with longtime customers.

Businessmen were asked if their business had any seasonal fluctuation. Below are their responses.

- 80% responded yes.
- 53% claimed fluctuation related to the farm cycle.
- 35% saw fluctuations due to the employment situation of their customers.

Bear in mind that over 53% of these businesses were dependent on the farm trade or from individuals working on farms. It is likely that a good number of those businessmen reporting "employment situation" fluctuations were similarly dependent upon harvest or other seasonal agricultural activities which generated increased payrolls. Overall, it is only stating the obvious to say that business in Fabens was strongly related to the strength of its agricultural community.

Businessmen were asked how they compared their prices with those of El Paso? Their responses are displayed below.

- No response: 30%
- It varies: 13%
- About the same: 27%
- Higher: 21%
- Lower: 9%

Perhaps comparing the prices of specific items between Fabens and El Paso businesses is more informative. In making these comparisons, only those items with the most constant consumption were chosen (see Table 7.3).

TABLE 7.3 Prices of Selected Food Items: Fabens and El Paso

Item	Fabens	El Paso
Bread	25	25
Eggs	41	39
Milk (1/2 gal.)	57	51
Hamburger	59	53
Chicken (cut up fryer)	43	31
Potatoes (per lb.)	15	12
Wheaties	52	43
Sugar, 5 lbs.	75	60
Crest toothpaste	65	43
Ivory soap	14	13
Band Aids	98	79

Source: Notre Dame Research Team.

Obviously, from the list of items in Table 7.3, it cost between 5 to 51% more to live in Fabens than in El Paso. The overall cost of living in Fabens, based on this small list of supplies was 21% more than living in nearby El Paso. It is not clear why it cost more to live in Fabens than in El Paso, but transporting and smaller amounts of basic supplies may have been important factors.

Businessmen were asked what they thought about Faben's future. Results were as follows:

- Improving: 25%
- "It depends": 5%
- Deteriorating: 50%
- Won't change: 20%

Interestingly, these responses did not represent one particular kind of business or businessman. It must also be added that no unqualified answers were provided. Those, for instance, who see Fabens surviving, or say "It depends," all implied that some change was needed, in wages, leadership, or diversification. Most of those who were pessimistic phrased their answers in such a way as to indicate that "if Fabens keeps up this way" it will decline thus exhibiting a desire for change. Few viewed the town as unalterable.

The Consumer

Two hundred questionnaires, in both English and Spanish, were sent to a cross section of townspeople. All totaled, 40 were returned: 23 in Spanish and 17 in English. Though these results must be taken cautiously due to the small return rate, they suggested a distinct pattern of the purchasing habits among Fabens' residents.

Residents purchased their everyday supplies in Fabens. About 70% of all groceries were purchased in Fabens. In addition, such sundry items as tobacco, razors, prescriptions, haircuts, and so forth, were also bought in Fabens. However, once we get beyond everyday needs, the proportion of goods bought locally dropped off dramatically. Residents tended to leave town for such services as dentists and doctors. Overall, 65% of those sampled say they leave Fabens for medical services. There were differences by ethnicity. Slightly over 50% of Anglos patronized the local physician, whereas only about 20% of Mexican Americans sought the assistance of local physicians. It should be noted, however, that the proclivity of Mexican Americans to seek medical assistance outside of Fabens may have been due to charity and to the medical care treatment available in El Paso hospitals.

Expensive, infrequently purchased items, tended to be purchased in El Paso or nearby Ysleta. Approximately 80% of Fabens' television sets, for instance, were purchased out of town, as were about 70% of all refrigerators. Of all appliances, only washing machines constituted important sales for Fabens merchants: half of the towns washers were purchased locally.

The entertainment industry in Fabens did poorly. Over 85% say that most of their entertainment dollars were spent outside Fabens. So negative, in fact, was Fabens' association with entertainment or leisure in the minds of its residents that over 80% of the town children's toys and playthings were purchased elsewhere.

As would be expected of low income people, lack of transportation likely accounted for the fact that overall, more Mexican Americans than Anglos shopped locally.

Two other questions were asked of the Fabens sample: "What does Fabens most lack?" and "What would it take to make you shop more in Fabens?" Respondents mentioned the lack of recreational facilities, such as movies, bowling, increase parlors, and others. Some mentioned the lack of farm-related services such as grain storage, new crops, better broker relationships, and so on. Three respondents mentioned the lack of hospital and ambulance services. To the question regarding what would make them shop more in Fabens, respondents mentioned "lower prices." Others mentioned greater variety within and among shops. Three respondents wanted to have a shopping center come to Fabens.

There were any number of things Fabens' businessmen could have done to attract Fabens' shoppers. Not the least would have been to upgrade the exterior and interiors of their stores. Most Fabens' stores look extremely shabby, and gave the impression of failure.

Businesses in Fabens were somewhat stable. There were no innovators among those remaining. The newest business, Delgado's pharmacy, replaced a drug store which failed several years before. Given the precarious nature of business in Fabens, most businessmen were unwilling to try anything innovative. They survived by taking few risks.

One recent incident was enlightening. Several businessmen decided that Fabens residents who worked in El Paso were spending much of their pay there. They felt that a considerable amount of money was being spent on Friday nights after paychecks had been cashed. A group of businessmen approached the bank and suggested that if the bank stayed open on Friday evenings, workers would return to Fabens and cash their checks. As a result, this would increase their spending in the town. The group suggested a trial period of several months. The bank board of directors refused to cooperate. The bank's decision had been reached with no research on the part of the bank into the actual numbers of Fabens townspeople who work or cash their checks in El Paso.

One businessman expressed the sentiment of many others: "I would have gone along with the experimental Friday night hours if the bank had. I could have juggled my hours. But by myself I really couldn't do anything here to rock the boat. This is too small a town for a boat rocker."

8

The Influentials

Community Leadership and Decision-Making

This chapter examines the use of power and decision-making in Fabens. Of particular concern is the existence of a "consensus group" of influentials in the community. We will frequently refer to these individuals as a "consensus group of influentials." Rather than imply conscious association and agreement among these elite individuals, consensus refers simply to the agreement among others as to who are influentials in the Fabens community. Such an agreement was arrived at by using several measurement techniques. Those men who are assigned the label "influential" by only one of the measurement techniques are known as independent influentials. Those designated by two or more techniques are referred to as "consensus influentials."

Three techniques for measuring influentials in Fabens are used: the reputational, the decision-making, and the interorganizational.

In studying the decision-making process, three important issues facing the community were assessed. The three issues were identified by asking a group of Fabens citizens what they viewed were the most important issues

The Yellow Rose, pages 79–98

that had occurred in Fabens over the past 10 years. Although most of the issues were addressed, discussions with other townspeople were also undertaken in order to gain a better understanding of the issues that had been identified as significant by respondents.

A second approach was to review 10 years of issues by the community's weekly newspaper. Results corroborated what had been reported by Faben's respondents as significant issues, with new issues also identified.

The Three Issues: A Discussion

The three issues chosen for analysis in this chapter were selected with very special reasons in mind. First, it was important that the selected issues reflected the concerns of several social strata in the Fabens community. Since Fabens may be divided into occupational (farmers vs. merchants, and both vs. laborers), ethnic (Mexican Americans vs. Anglos), and religious (Catholic vs. Protestant) sectors, it was necessary that the selected issues reflected this diversity.

In the history section, we discussed in great detail the farm workers' strikes that had occurred in the past. No evidence of strikes or of direct class-oriented issues were uncovered for the period of this research. In fact, there seemed to be widespread concern about the declining cotton economy and what this had meant to farmers and to small businessmen. In fact, such a concern was tied to the lack of union organizing or of a politically effective voluntary organization of any kind among workers. It is therefore not surprising that the economic issues that were uncovered failed to be defined in class terms.

A primary reason for undertaking the Fabens community study was the severe economic crises facing farmers and local businessmen. Thus, two issues to be raised concern the business and farming sectors. The third issue was the community committee delegated with the task of inviting the Notre Dame Research group to Fabens. In any event, a list of specific areas addressed in this chapter is presented in Table 8.1.

Attempts by Fabens to Attract Industry

In 1958, a group of about 63 Fabens' businessmen formed a group with the objective of improving the local economy. Initially, the objective was to attract nonfarming industry to the area with the hope of creating jobs for Fabens residents. Each member of the group contributed approximately $60, and a section of land was purchased (in 1969 the land included the

TABLE 8.1 The Major Issues Which Have Attracted the Time and Energy of Fabens Community Leaders During the Period 1950–1970

1	The incorporation of Fabens
2	Decline of cotton agriculture as the base of the community economy
3	Purchasing of the water company by the sewer district in 1963
4	The school board in 1969
5	Opening of the Fabens golf course
6	Organization of the Fabens Development Corporation
7	The El Paso Valley Development Corporation
8	The Cotton Producers Institute
9	Fabens Community Study Project by Notre Dame
10	The opening of a community swimming pool
11	Agee's "Tex-Togs" company
12	Businesses staying open on Friday nights
13	Border clothing factory that went out of business
14	The merchants' baseball park
15	The Hicks-Ponder plant

Source: Notre Dame Research Team.

Hicks-Ponder and Ellis Chevrolet properties). The group called itself the Fabens Development Corporation (FDC). Ben Powell was named president of the original board; E. B. Pinkerton, J. N. Hendricks, Barney Franklin, Grady Walden, William Summers, and James Surratt were said to be especially active in forming the corporation.

The corporation purchased 20 acres of land at $20 per acre. The area did not include roads or water. It straddled Fabens Street, and at a later date W. B. Ellis purchased about half of the land at $500 per acre. Ellis proceeded to build his auto agency on the property, and, at a later date, the county repaved and improved Fabens Street. The relationship between the Development Corporation, Ellis' purchase of the land, and the county's improvement of Fabens Street was never made clear, and seemed very suspicious.

An early attempt to bring industry to Fabens, following the formation of the FDC was an effort at bringing Tex-Togs to the community. Tex-Togs was owned by a Mr. Guy Agee, and it is unclear how the FDC and Mr. Agee connected.

Tex-Togs was an EL Paso-based firm which sold a considerable proportion of its products to Sears, Roebuck. In 1957, Agee and the FDC connected. Agee wanted to start a sewing factory in Fabens and agreed to put up half of all the costs of a factory. (There are several opinions on this, though it is most likely that he wanted all of the building to be paid for by the FDC. In fact, an El Paso firm drew up a perspective of a plant which would cost about $50,000 to build. Elevations and plans were actually drawn up.) The money was to come from the El Paso Valley Compress, and a number of meetings were held between Agee, Ben Powell, and Vickers Sr. Apparently, Sears was willing to guarantee purchase of the Fabens made products and the Compress was thus guaranteed repayment of the money it had put up for the factory. W. R. Summers made a trip to Chicago, Sears's headquarters, in 1957 and again in 1958 in order to discuss the details with Sears's executives. By Summers's second trip, Agee was reportedly asking the FDC to put up not only the factory, but in addition, to finance the machinery. According to Ben Powell, the "tab" was now up to $150,000. At this point, the FDC began to hesitate. Agee decided to back out and the entire deal fell through.

At a later date, the FDC was successful in an attempt to attract industry to the area. Casual contacts with El Paso businessmen indicated that additional sewing facilities were needed; El Paso firms could job-out garments and garment parts. The Fabens Building Corporation (FBC) was formed independently of the FDC, though there was some overlap of membership. A Mr. Hicks (no relation to Hicks-Ponder) began operation in Fabens in an existing building (a former bowling alley) provided by the FBC and partially stocked by it. Hicks himself provided much of the funds. Approximately 40 women were employed at peak work. The company failed shortly after. At least $50,000 in debts were left, and were covered by friends of Hicks. Both Ben Powell and Leroy Creek attempted to find buyers for the sewing machines.

Mr. Ponder, of Hicks-Ponder, was identified as a possible buyer of the sewing machines. Hicks-Ponder bought the machines. Later a lease was taken on the small building so as to attract competition, as one businessman put it. Indeed, Ben Powell claimed that once the lease was drawn and the machinery sold, no less than five subsequent inquiries were made by other manufacturers. Regardless of the sale and the lease, FBC members lost their initial $400 investments on the failure of the original Hicks plant.

Hicks-Ponder subsequently became interested in establishing a larger operation in Fabens. The FDC suggested that it would donate the remainder of its desert acreage across from Ellis Chevrolet, provided that Hicks-Ponder construct a building on the site and employ local residents. This was agreed upon, pursuant to Fabens' providing sufficient water. The water board refurbished a tank near the expressway and provided an 8-inch main.

Hicks-Ponder built the plant and imported a manager from another area of Texas. The plant, however, conducted only research and hired but one or two Fabens residents. Merger of Hicks-Ponder with Blue Bell Clothing further postponed the promised beginning of manufacturing at the plant. As of August 1969, the plant still did no manufacturing.

Several things stand out in discussing the attempts at industrializing Fabens. First, though the efforts had not been successful, fault cannot be placed on those who worked at attracting industry to Fabens. Rather, the main problem was the climate and character of Fabens itself and the relationships among those attempting to industrialize the community. As a private and informally tied group, they had limited access to facilities and aid to any prospective plant. They—and Fabens—had no power. Secondly, there were the interactions among various sectors of the community, each with its own interests. Nonagricultural business was involved. Agribusiness, in the form of the Compress was certainly actively involved, and indeed, was prepared to put its own money into a sewing shop. The county was involved in road improvement. The water board was involved in establishing a new tank and furnishing water to a new company. The bank was involved in seeking purchasers for equipment.

Regardless of the level of involvement, the focus was in creating jobs for women. Why? The answer appears to reflect the power wielded by agriculture in the community. One large farmer, when asked whether he would favor industry in Fabens replied:

> It would depend on the type and size of the industry... From a laboring standpoint, it's got to be in balance. Now you have all agriculture and no industry. Don't go to the other extreme. It would be a lot better to have a related business, such as a packing plant, that would benefit the farmers and the businessmen.

Another large farmer gave his opinion:

> Industry won't work by itself. We farmers need men we can count on because when irrigation water comes we have to take it. You can't go running around at 2:00 a.m. some morning looking for men to help out. Industry would take these men away from us. Now if we could just get those Mexicans coming across to work in the fields for us, well, OK, we could use factories then...

It is thus not surprising that attempts at industrializing Fabens should reflect the farmer's view—if it were not linked directly to farming, new businesses should hire only women. Perhaps the most interesting admission came from the influential farmer quoted above. When asked about progress for Fabens, he replied:

> If a boom came to Fabens, a few nearby farmers might gain in the rise of property values. But that's all. A boom means tourists and picnickers. Beer cans and blocked roads. Farmers and people don't mix...

As a non-incorporated community, with no system of checks and balances each group could exert its own influence, or make idiosyncratic decisions without concern for others in the community. In a sense, Fabens was like a set of little fiefdoms—each fiefdom fighting for its own view and livelihood. The Fabens Golf Course is yet another example. In this area, the water board exerted considerable influence. Many Fabens residents claimed that the original golf course dried out and died because the water commissioner refused to provide water to the golf course at a minimal charge. The county represented by Rogelio Sanchez, had agreed to furnish the labor, but the commissioner, James Ethridge, "would shut the water off when the workers wanted to irrigate the course." Many believed that a personal vendetta was behind Ethridge's action—Sanchez having previously unseated Ethridge's father as county commissioner. Regardless of the reasons, the golf course, ostensibly a community park for all Fabens residents, faded away.

While well intentioned, the attempts to bring industry to Fabens were not well planned and this led to many problems. For example, the Compress's offer of $50,000 could have been purely altruistic or it could have been made because of the potentially good return on a $50,000 Tex-Togs investment. At the same time, the Compress represents farmers, and many farmers looked with favor upon the need trades which employed women and which theoretically resulted in contented males who were more likely to stay put and be available for farm work. In addition, if laborers' wives can earn salaries, the low salary farm workers earn, according to this line of reasoning, was much more likely to be accepted. Non-agribusiness, doubtless, assumed that people tend to shop where they are paid, and thus an increase in local payrolls would benefit local merchants. Essentially, however, such an assumption was short-sighted and unrealistic. The needle trades pay exceptionally low wages and border areas such as the El Paso Valley have proven ideal sources of cheap labor; however, a 1968 report prepared for the U.S. Department of Commerce on the employment and industrial potential of the United States–Mexico border region states that needle trades were only an interim industry and face bleak futures. Needle shops moved on to Singapore, Hong Kong, and others, as unionism and increased wages pushed sewing costs up beyond acceptable profit margins. So sewing shops would appear to have been a weak foundation upon which to build long-term prosperity in the community.

Efforts to Combat the Plight of the Cotton Industry

Many factors must be considered when discussing the decline of cotton agriculture as a basis of the Fabens economy. For example, two men interviewed had different opinions about the future of the cotton industry. One individual, although somewhat dejected about the decline of the industry, felt it would recover its losses. Another respondent, however, was very pessimistic about the industry's future. The decline, he felt, would continue. The latter individual also happened to be one of the largest farmers in the area, and was part owner of a local feed lot. He was one of the lucky few whose farm was large enough so that he could diversify his investments. The crucial point was that he moved his money away from its dependence on cotton.

Some individuals felt that the key to reversing the decline in cotton agriculture was to simply sell more cotton. The farmers' success lay in acquiring a better price for cotton or to sell in greater volume.

The decline itself was caused by the increased use of synthetic materials by domestic mills. The cotton industry failed to mount a campaign promoting the benefits of cotton and was now suffering the consequences. They nonetheless agreed that it had been the efforts of the National Cotton Council in recent years which had enabled cotton to hold its own. In Fabens, the organization which had done most to promote cotton was the Rio Valley Women's Club's annual Cotton Festival. The festival is capped by a ball, in which local girls (all Anglo girls, incidentally) compete for the honor of being Cotton Maid, and all are sponsored by clubs. At best, national and local promotional efforts had served to stabilize the demand for cotton, but had not succeeded in increasing its demand.

In addition, to the use of synthetic materials, the cotton decline was exacerbated in the Southwest by the ending of the Bracero program. The Bracero program allowed farmers to make use of cheap Mexican labor, who worked in the United States but remained citizens of Mexico. When the program ended (around 1963), farm costs escalated and most farmers began using machines.

A third factor that contributed to the decline of cotton was the involvement of the U.S. government. As one individual said, "If the government would have stayed out of it (e.g., paying people not to plant cotton, guaranteeing people so much land, etc.), we'd be in a hell of a lot better shape."

Others felt that the best ways to reverse cotton's decline was to first support the Cotton Producers Institute, and, secondly, make everyone who depended on cotton be an advocate. This proposal, of course, pointed to the crucial importance of national and local promotion campaigns.

The Cotton Producers Institute (C.P.I.) is a national organization which was started about 1964 or 1965, with the objective of researching new ways in which cotton could be used and in promoting the cotton industry.

The response to the institute was poor until its support was mandatory. Farmers were required to give $1.00 per bale of cotton they produced to the C.P.I. (If this created a burden on the farmer, he could request a refund.) In 1969, the institute was in its infancy and not close to achieving its goals.

Several important cotton farmers foresaw a bleak future for cotton, and didn't hide their pessimism. They considered the decline irreversible, a fact that "just happen[s] in business." While they supported the C.P.I., they didn't think anything would reverse cotton's decline. About the best they could hope for would be to stabilize the situation.

Cotton could be produced inexpensively in other parts of the world (e.g., Mexico, India, the South American countries, and Egypt) with very cheap labor. Farmers argued that "with our high cost here in the United States, we just can't compete." "Farmers here are broke." They acknowledged that labor won't get cheaper and mourned that "profits are zero in the cotton business." Given these circumstances, they saw no hope for the future of cotton.

Many small farmers were following family tradition by raising cotton, but many were inclined to abandon the tradition. Small farmers had to think about what they could grow or do as farmers in order to make a profit. One of the more successful farmers offered the following thoughts:

> Diversification isn't approached rightly here because people go at it on an individual basis. The big farmers like myself can diversify, but the smaller farmers can't because they need big capital. It's got to be done in a community fashion. You have to create a cooperative . . . More diversification spirals into many other benefits.

Several others felt that Fabens should consolidate and focus its attention on one project. Opinion was divided, however. One farmer thought that perhaps he was the person who could bring all the conflicting groups together. One man thought about managing a cooperative at a salary of over $25,000 per year. He discovered, however, "two individuals would both be willing to do something until the two came together. [Then] the friction would dissolve things." He was physically threatened several times, and finally gave up on the idea. As he summed it up, "We need somebody new to come in here and do something. We're so close together, we don't know how far apart we are."

Many of the farmers felt that if new industry was to thrive in Fabens, it would have to be industry that would help both the town and the agricultural community. Examples ranged from packing plants to a spinning mill. Although most people didn't show his cynicism, they did agree with one matter-of-fact analysis: "You people [the Notre Dame Study Group] are coming in here trying to get more money for the farm workers, but the farmers just don't have it to give."

The El Paso Valley Cotton Association (EPVCA) was a regional organization geared primarily to the needs of the farming community. A. R. Miller was the president of the association, which basically represented the Valley in Washington. In February or March of 1969, Tex Barron, then the manager of the EPVCA, and the members of that organization had concurred that the Valley needed a survey that would assist them in making a decision about what kinds of businesses farmers should pursue. The next important issue was whether the survey could be conducted through the association—the EPVCA—or whether the survey should be conducted under the auspices of a new association or corporation. The latter approach was preferred because EPVCA was strictly a farmer's organization, whereas a new organization would represent broader concerns—both businessmen and farmers. The new organization was formed and named the El Paso Valley Development Company (EPVDC).

Shortly thereafter, there was a meeting among the gins in the Valley, the oil mills, and some banks. These organizations pledged some money for speculative purposes. (Each group was informed that there was an attempt to bring in industry that would benefit both the farming and business communities in Fabens.)

While a number development organizations were organized, they tended to be exclusionary rather than inclusive. The EPVDC is an example of the type of community organization that Fabens farmers and small businessmen had been attempting to develop for some time. Townspeople and farmers were working together in an effort to solve some of the problems facing the Fabens community. Both the FDC and the FBC overrepresented the business sector of the community. The EPVDC, while bringing together the business and farm leaders of the Valley, never considered the possibility that the laborers, primarily Mexican Americans, should participate in the planning of various projects. Old habits are hard to die.

Fabens' Decision to Invite the Notre Dame for the Community Study Group

Father Getz had conducted various community organization studies himself since his arrival in Fabens in 1966. He had devised a program, which he sent to major foundations in November of 1968 (e.g., Rockefeller, Carnegie, Ford) requesting funds for research support. Unfortunately, funding was not forthcoming because foundations were not interested in funding community studies such as Getz was proposing. Getz then planned to direct his own project with the assistance of about four or five college students from University of Texas at El Paso (UTEP) working for him during the summer.

Getz wrote to most of the businessmen in Fabens asking for their cooperation. The letters were written on church stationery, thus associating the project with Getz who was becoming increasingly unpopular at that time. Jesse Daffron,Jr. and Davis Holdman Jr. persuaded Father Getz to abandon the hiring of local college students and concentrate upon obtaining researchers from an outside organization with the experience and prestige to handle such a project.

Jesse Daffron Jr., who had attended Notre Dame and had worked for Dr. D'Antonio in the latter's follow-up study in El Paso in 1962, contacted D'Antonio, and sent him a copy of Getz's community study proposal. This was actually how the formal contact with Notre Dame was initiated. D'Antonio was scheduled to lecture at UTEP in mid April and agreed to come early and discuss the matter with Getz, Daffron, and others who would be interested. Following this meeting, at which D'Antonio sketched out a possible community study, the idea was discussed at a parish council meeting. At some point, wider community representation had to be obtained. It was, in fact, Monsignor Quinn of El Paso who suggested that the parish council "throw a supper" for the businessmen in order to get the community involved. Individuals invited to the dinner were:

Jess Daffron Sr.	Jess Daffron Jr.
Rogelio Sanchez	Monsignor Quinn
Leroy Creek	Father Getz
Manuel Provencio	Charles Calhoun
Davis Lee Holdman Jr.	W. B. Ellis

All but Calhoun and Ellis were able to attend the meeting. "It was a fiasco," commented one of the organizers. "The guests took a look at those invited, claimed there were not sufficient sectors of the community present to represent all ideas and suggested a postponement for a year." Both Daffron

Jr. and Holdman Jr. pushed for a second meeting with wider representation at a much earlier date. In fact, 2 weeks later the first "formal" meeting was called and those who attended formed the *Fabens Advisory Committee.* Monsignor Quinn had already given the parish permission to pledge $5,000 of its money for the study. Present at this meeting were: Father Getz, Davis Lee Holdman Jr., Jess Daffron Jr., Ben Powell, Earl Drake, Manuel Provencio, Leory Creek, Dr. Vilorio, Alex Fierro, Martin Lettunich, and Otis DeVolin.

At this meeting Getz adamantly claimed the study was not "his," not a "Catholic study," and so forth, but a study to benefit the community. Getz then dissociated himself from the matter. Perhaps because of this the group agreed to the study. More importantly, they agreed to associate themselves with the project.

When the R. F. K Institute at Notre Dame donated $15,000, the foundation for the project had been laid. In addition to this total of $20,000, the university ultimately provided in-kind aid totaling close to $10,000 and Dr. Julian Samora of Notre Dame provided an additional $1,000 from his Mexican Border Study project.

Some individuals acknowledge that a key factor in getting the proposal passed was the prospect of the economic development it would bring to Fabens in the future. Others thought it was that local farmers and businessmen didn't have to pay for the study. The townspeople "want something for nothing... many people around here don't have the foresight to see the benefits for the future of spending money on projects like this in the present will bring."

What did the townspeople expect the Notre Dame team to accomplish? Perhaps three things. First, residents of Fabens would be informed about their community. It was clear from the interviews that were conducted that many residents knew very little about recent events affecting the community and even less about the community's history. Second, the proposed study was to serve as a legitimizing agent. One businessman said as much. "This is why we have Notre Dame on the ball, so they can convince some of those big Eastern corporations what we can do for them." Another felt that "if we [the Notre Dame group] went back North and brought down a factory that would employ about 300 people and bring a payroll into Fabens he'd be happy." Thus, the Notre Dame report was seen as a way to reveal the attractiveness of Fabens to potential industrial investors. A third reason why Notre Dame was invited to Fabens, at least in the townspeople's eyes, was the evaluative function. Although they realized the ultimate choices in any of these issues was up to them, many of the townspeople appeared interested in suggestions they could agree upon.

The Community Leadership Structure

Concentrating on the community leadership structure, the reputational, issue-decision, and IOL techniques were used to measure the visibility among Fabens leaders.

Reputation, as a factor for attaining influence, is a fundamental indicator of visibility. Using a seven-point scale of influence, which was collapsed to three categories of high, medium, and low influence, respondents were asked to nominate six individuals as possessing high to moderate influence. These data are presented in Table 8.2.

The list is interesting because the top six individuals represent very distinct sub-groupings in the community. Mike Maros and Charles Calhoun for example were among the biggest farmers in the Fabens area. Ben Powell, the biggest vote getter at 65%, and Leroy Creek were two prominent and well-liked businessmen. Rogelio Sanchez was a county official, and especially important in this study because he was the first Mexican American to hold a county political position in the Fabens district. The last of the "top reputed influentials" in Fabens was Father Getz, the pastor of the town's only Catholic Church. His importance in the community power structure stemmed from the fact that 85% of the population of Fabens was Mexican American, and almost all were followers of the Catholic religion.

At the time of the study, Father Getz had only been in Fabens for 3 years but had stirred up sharp controversy among the Anglo population. Getz's sin, so to speak, were his attempts at helping the Mexican-American

TABLE 8.2 Ratings of the Top Reputed Influential in Fabens in a 7-Point Scale of Influence in Initiation, Supporting, or Shaping Actions Which Have the Most Effect in the Community

	High Influence	Moderate Influence	Low Influence	Total Influence
Mike Maros, Farmer	44	12	0	56
Ben Powell, Insurance, Real Estate	41	24	6	71
Rogelio Sanchez, County Commissioner	38	9	3	50
Father Getz, Pastor, R. C. Church	29	6	0	35
Leroy Creek, Bank President	24	24	0	48
Charles Calhoun, Farm Manager	9	24	3	36
W. B. Ellis, Owner, Chevrolet Franchise	6	18	6	30
Manuel Provencio, Gas Station Owner	6	21	0	27
Baker Ethridge	6	15	6	27

Source: Notre Dame Research Team.

population by encouraging them for greater educational achievement, and to take initiative in taking town leadership positions. Powerful Anglo leadership saw his efforts as moving him beyond the realm of religious commitment to the sphere of politics, where they didn't think he belonged. In reality, Getz was challenging the prevailing racial stratification system and was a threat to the status quo.

Visibility refers to the degree to which an actor is perceived influential by others. Another index of visibility was to ascertain who was most active in Fabens. Those persons who had been involved to any degree in at least eight (or over half) of the fifteen major community issues examined in this study were designated as the "most involved" leaders. These data are presented in Table 8.3.

Of the eight most active men, four had also been designated as top reputed influentials. These were Ben Powell, Rogelio Sanchez, Charles Calhoun, and Leroy Creek. It is important to note that the fifteen major issues examined were more important to the business community, as opposed to the farming sector of Fabens. Only three of the issues were directly related to farming, whereas the remaining twelve were primarily involved with "town affairs." This is an important finding because it highlights the focus of planning for the future of the community, and farming was only represented by one person.

The crucial question is "Why were town leaders involved in four times as many different major issues as were farming community leaders?" One

TABLE 8.3 Respondents Most Involved in Fifteen Major Community Issues

	Very Involved (1)	Moderately Involved (2)	Little Involvement (3)	Total Number Issues Involved (1 + 2 + 3)	Not Involved (4)
Ben Powell	10	2	0	12	3
Earl Drake[a]	8	2	1	11	3
Rogelio Sanchez	7	3	2	12	3
W. B. Ellis	5	4	5	14	1
Manuel Provencio[a]	5	2	2	9	5
James Ethridge	5	1	3	9	6
Charles Clhoun	4	3	1	8	7
Leroy Creek[a]	3	4	2	9	5

[a] These totals add up to fourteen because these men were interviewed before the fifteenth issue was added to the list.

explanation was that the decline of cotton agriculture, the foundation of the Fabens economy, was an issue. And when cotton was hitched to a large number of related issues, it provided business influentials greater opportunity to become involved. A narrow focus of issues would have limited participation by other members of the community. Also, the ideology attached to farming stresses individualism, which strongly biased farmers against collective action. Consequently, farmers had some difficulty competing in and adapting to an organized social system (Lenski, 1966, pp. 382–386). In this light, farmers of Fabens were typical, as were members of the business sector—that is, very much involved in community affairs because their businesses were dependent on the community.

In Fabens, seven individuals held executive positions in five or more major community organizations. Only one of these seven men, Mike Maros, was on a previous list, but note that all seven of the men possessing the strongest interorganizational ties were farmers by occupation. These men were moderately involved (about four issues each) in community issues, and, except for Mike Maros, were rated low on reputational power. They did, however, have access to power through a network they developed over time. See Table 8.4 for a list of the major organizations.

The decisional and interorganizational techniques used in this study produced strikingly different results. Whereas the four new influentials uncovered by the issue-involvement index were all businessmen, the six new influentials found through the interorganizational index were farmers. Both techniques, therefore, uncovered mutually exclusive sets of independent influentials.

It is even more surprising to note that five of the six top reputed influentials (with the exception of Father Getz) were included in one or the other, but not both, of the groups derived by the decisional and interorganizational techniques. It would not be unreasonable to label these six persons "consensus influentials" because they derived their influence by both reputation and by either the decisional or interorganizational measures. In contrast, independent influentials are those who were identified as being in the top category of influentials by only one measure.

To clarify again, then, the six-man consensus group of influentials uncovered when measuring visibility were the top reputed influentials, all of whom had high status positions in the community, and five of whom were designated as either most involved in issues or as independents. These men were more visible than independent influentials who were mentioned by only one index of community power.

TABLE 8.4 Community Organizations in Fabens to Which Influentials Belong[a]
The Fabens Bank
El Paso Valley Compress
Fabens Cotton Delinting Plant
Fabens Cotton Gin
Lions Club
Masonic Lodge
Project Bravo
Rio Valley Women's Club
Fabens School Board
Tornillo Cotton Oil Company
Tornillo Gin Company
Fabens Development Corporation
El Paso Valley Development Corporation
El Paso Valley Cotton Association
Southwestern Irrigated Growers Association
League of United Latin American Citizens (LULAC)
The Volunteers Fire Department

[a]These include business, civic, and related organizations.

Note: Persons were considered as being in "executive positions" in these organizations if they held an office within the organization, served on the governing board, or where relevant, owned at least 100 shares of stock in one of these organizations.

At this point, we can introduce additional data to strengthen the results discussed above. In a sense, it is an exercise in sensitivity analysis. As one check on visibility, respondents were probed to identify leaders in the following social institutions in Fabens: community sectors as education, religious, business, and farming. Mike Maros and Charles Calhoun were seen as the most influential in the agricultural sector; Father Getz in the religious—he also received more votes than anyone regardless of sector; Leroy Creek and Ben Powell were seen as influential in the business sector; and Mr. Ericson as most influential in the education sector (he was the superintendent of the Fabens school system). Note that five of the six men thought to have the most influence in these sectors also were top reputed influentials. Unfortunately, respondents were not also asked who possessed the most influence in the political sector, but if this question had been posed, Rogelio Sanchez would almost certainly have been chosen. Thus, responses to this question provides further support for persons identified as consensus influentials. In addition to occupying formal positions of influence, being the top reputed influentials, and being “most involved,” they also were the most influential men in their individual sectors.

Discussion

In most cases, leaders in Fabens were property owners or managers of businesses, the majority of which were related in some way to the cotton industry which had dominated life in Fabens. In fact, only Father Getz and Rogelio Sanchez did not represent agribusiness interests in the Fabens leadership structure.

In his position as pastor of the Catholic church, Father Getz had made it possible to develop a base of influence in the community simply because such a large percentage of the community were Catholic. But more significantly in terms of the power base which Father Getz had developed, was that such a large number of these people were Catholic, Mexican American, and poor. Our data support the proposition that Father Getz, more than anyone else in the community, had tried to represent the interests of Mexican Americans, the largest group, in Fabens.

Rogelio Sanchez's position was more complicated—he certainly stood as a representative of Mexican Americans in some symbolic way since he was the first of their ethnic group to be elected to a county office in this region. He represented, moreover, the classic example of a local person who was succeeded within the system and who commanded the sympathies of at least the middle class and older Mexican Americans. His power base seemed to be related both to his political position and to his ethnicity.

The lack of labor union organizations or of any strong neighborhood organizations among the poor in Fabens had prevented the emergence of a strong leadership from within their ranks. Consequently, their voice is conspicuously absent within the leadership structure of Fabens.

Issues that arose in the community were associated with individuals possessing money and prestige. The very structure of a border farming community with the traditions of labor and ethnic exploitation that had marked Fabens and hundreds of other communities in the Southwest, further mitigated against the development of a broad-based community leadership structure. Because the poor lacked a voice in the decision-making processes, it is not surprising that issues focusing on the interests of those in the middle and upper income brackets continued to hold the attention among Fabens leaders.

Also, it should be noted that a majority of Fabens community leaders believed that the major issue facing Fabens was job creation. It seems clear, however, that the interest of leaders in the community lay in maintaining or recovering their own income levels rather than manifesting an altruist concern about basic changes in the social life of Fabens.

There was much inequality in Fabens. Moreover, few had sought ways to resolve the many problems that arose from such social and economic inequality. In one sense, leaders in Fabens said they had been doing their best at trying to improve the economic and social climate in the community. But in reality, little action had taken place on improving the situation—for example, the resodding and development of the Fabens Golf Course, it became clear how this action served only well-heeled in the community. By midsummer of 1970, the Fabens Golf Course was being used almost exclusively by the Anglo members of the community. The action to improve the golf course exemplified the degree to which community leaders and wealthy in Fabens have failed at finding ways to bridge the gap between the majority of people in the community and the minority who enjoyed most of the community's facilities.

A second factor of social inequality in Fabens was the question of incorporation. Incorporation would have provided many significant advantages for the community, writ large. But as has been shown, not all of Fabens's citizens are equally represented. In terms of class and ethnicity, the poor and near poor, and Mexican Americans, their interests were underrepresented. There were no checks and balances; once decisions were made they were final and tended to favor the privileged in the community.

Farming interests in Fabens were powerful. Farmers had a problem with incorporation: an incorporated Fabens would have an overwhelming Mexican-American citizenry. Their vote, in fact, could have determined whether incorporation would take place at all. But they did not have the resources or experience to make incorporation work. While Rogelio Sanchez, Judge Rueda, and Manuel Provencio provided important links between the community leadership structure and the Mexican-American middle class, Father Getz formed the most notable link with the lower class. And, there appeared to be no individual representing the Anglo lower class.

One obvious way to proceed, would be for the present leaders of Fabens to form a coalition that would advocate for incorporating Fabens and then take over the offices and run the community. Gradually, some Mexican Americans might have been expected to occupy important leadership positions in the local government. An alternative would have been for the same coalition of community leaders to determine that it would be in the long-term interest of everyone to find and help develop the indigenous leadership among Mexican Americans, and to set specific goals by which they would then move into important government positions. It was not in the interest of the community to avoid this question. What were the attitudes expressed by community leaders towards some of these questions?

Among the 34 leaders who were interviewed, 15 favored incorporation. Eight were uncertain or had no definite view on the subject, and slightly less than a third opposed incorporation. Among those favoring incorporating Fabens, nearly all stated a willingness to join a committee in promoting incorporation or to hold discussions with others in an attempt to convince Fabens residents about the benefits of incorporation. Those who favored incorporation represented less than the complete spectrum of sectors in the leadership structure. There was, therefore, a somewhat narrow base for those wishing to promote incorporation.

A majority of the leaders believed that Fabens would not be able to resolve its problems, and that it required outside assistance. A large portion of this majority believed that assistance would come from the Federal government and that it would be extensive. A small number thought that Fabens might be able to solve its problems with only a minimum amount of State and Federal assistance. About one third of the leaders thought Fabens could solve its own problems.

Though the leadership in Fabens agreed that the community did not have the resources necessary to solve its own problems, they were not enthusiastic about some of the possible solutions that were being suggested in Washington. A majority of Fabens leaders were either opposed to Federal welfare payment programs for the unemployed or opposed guaranteed minimum incomes for all families. The responses to both questions showed that one in six or one in seven favored these programs. What the leadership in Fabens sought was attracting industry to Fabens. If these responses suggest antipathy toward such Federal government programs, it would be difficult to set up these programs in Fabens, though they could make significant differences in the quality of life for many families in Fabens.

There is a hypocrisy involved this anti-government sentiment. Individuals favoring continued government subsidy of farm land, government cash payments to farmers in lieu of their actually using their farm lands for cash crops, did not favor guaranteed minimum incomes for all families. The main thrust of their objection was the idea that because people would be getting something for nothing it would tend to destroy their initiative. This logical dissonance had clearly escaped many anti-government opponents.

Leaders were asked a series of questions about the status of the Mexican-American population in Fabens. Two out of three thought it necessary to have Mexican-American leaders in Fabens, while less than one fifth objected to thinking of leaders in terms of ethnicity. Two out of three thought that in the past 2 years the number of potential Mexican-American leaders had increased. Others felt the leadership potential had remained stable over this period.

When asked what they thought would be necessary to realize this potential, their responses tended to be fragmentary. The largest single number (6) mentioned higher education. Other respondents thought that the potential leadership was actually being activated or that there was a natural process by which Mexican-American leaders would emerge.

The data indicate that the current group of Fabens leaders were not opposed to the development of Mexican-American leadership. At the same time, not a single person mentioned the possibility or importance of helping to develop this leadership. They tended, rather, to accept the so-called inevitable processes: either natural processes or higher education as the means by which Mexican Americans would eventually take leaderships roles in the community. (Unfortunately, data were not gathered on the higher education background of Anglo leadership in the community.)

In a separate series of interviews carried out with 11 Mexican Americans of mixed class status (working and middle), there was almost unanimous opinion (9 of 10) that it was necessary to have Mexican-American leaders in Fabens. One respondent expressed the feeling of all: "The town doesn't have any Latin inspiration. The youth don't have any example or 'reference' to look to. They need leaders that give us examples—also to give more voice to the Latin." Another expressed view was:

> Yes, it is necessary because the Anglos are now in control of everything. With the influence of Mexican-American leaders the people will benefit more. If you have someone who would fight for us, it would be good. If industry hasn't entered here, it is because the Anglo Americans don't want to lose their workers.

We asked members of the 11 Mexican American community sample an open-ended question requesting that they name the most influential persons in Fabens, and the list may be found below:

Rogelio Sanchez, County Commissioner (9)
Father Getz, Pastor, Catholic Church (4)
Mike Maros, Farm owner (4)
Jack Strickland, Businessman (3)
Earl Drake (3)
T. Rodriquez (3)

Judge G. G. Rueda, Justice of the Peace (3)
Ernesto Ramos (3)
Gilberto Rueda (3)
M. Provencio (3)
Harold Ivey, Farm owner (3)

Of the eleven persons to whom Mexican Americans gave three or more votes as the most influential in Fabens, only three persons received four or more votes. These were also among the consensus influentials that were identified by the Mexican-American community. Mexican Americans were as likely to name Mexican Americans as influentials as were Anglos. Thus out of the 38 persons receiving one, two, or three votes, 18 were Anglos and 20 were Mexican Americans. This contrast between voting patterns of the Mexican Americans and the formal community leaders suggests again the wide gap that existed between those who had power in Fabens and those who may have in fact come closer to representing the silent majority in the community.

9

Wealth, Poverty, and Ideology in Fabens

"Equality, Liberty, and the Pursuit of Happiness," the American creed, is an important myth of American culture, and one that has some difficulty in interpretation. In this chapter, I examine the extent to which Fabens residents acknowledged the reality of the American creed.

Most known societies have systems of values, norms, and so forth, which guide social behavior. In America, the cornerstone of this system is the American creed. The creed is passed on from one generation to the next through the family and through other social institutions such as the educational system. The creed stresses that America is a democracy of equality, where hard work is rewarded, rather than one's family name. However, because America is also characterized by much inequality, there are many opportunities to question the legitimacy of its creed.

This chapter seeks answers to two questions:

1. Was there a relationship between socioeconomic status and how individuals evaluated Fabens?
2. Were there differences by ethnicity in this evaluation?

The Yellow Rose, pages 99–113

Seven questions were asked of respondents in an effort to obtain well-rounded answers to both questions.

1. Fabens as a place to live and work.
2. Perceptions about opportunity structures in Fabens.
3. Perceptions about political opportunity structures in Fabens.
4. Concerns about income and economic security in Fabens.
5. Factors of wealth and poverty.
6. Wealth and poverty in Fabens.
7. Ethnicity, mobility, and occupation.

Fabens as a Place to Live and Work

The problems affecting Fabens were similar to those affecting other communities throughout America, such as unemployment, civil disorders, and welfare services. Table 9.1 displays the perceptions respondents had about the four most serious problems in Fabens. Unemployment and housing facilities were particularly bothersome to Fabens residents. Though all three income groups' viewed unemployment as a serious problem, the wealthy were least concerned and the middle class exhibited the greatest concern. Many among the middle income group and the poor mentioned the lack of industry in the community as an important factor influencing high unemployment. According to both classes, the development of an industrial plant in the area would reduce unemployment.

TABLE 9.1 Serious Problems Facing Fabens by Race and Hispanic Origin

	Unemployment	Housing Facilities	Violence/ Civil Disorder	Health Welfare
Income				
Poor	8	65	24	43
Middle	88	76	20	50
Rich	60	40	10	30
% of Total	**81**	**67**	**21**	**43**
Ethnicity				
Mexican-American	83	68	23	47
Anglo	67	67	8	37
% of Total	**79**	**67**	**19**	**45**

Source: Notre Dame Research Team

The middle income group showed the greatest degree of concern about housing facilities, and the rich the least. Two thirds of the poor also believed that housing was a serious problem. Though this finding was not surprising, the percentage was lower than might have been expected given the crowded conditions in which so many lived.

The middle income group was particularly sensitive to problems of health and welfare, and again, the rich expressed the least concern about these issues. The middle income group was especially concerned about the absence of a hospital in the community. As it stood, individuals with serious medical problems had to travel to El Paso or Isleta in order to receive care. At the other end of the spectrum, the rich tended to consider welfare services a serious problem only if they existed at all. The poor considered it a problem of insufficiency and the lack of Federal assistance to the poor.

The three economic groups also differed, but only slightly, on matters of violence and civil disorder. The poor tended to express slightly greater concern than either the middle or upper income groups because crime was more likely to occur in their own neighborhoods. The overall response for all three income groups, however, suggested a low concern with these issues. Several economically poor respondents complained about broken windows or about the destruction of their possessions. One respondent complained, "I can never leave my house alone."

With the exception of this last problem, civil disorder and violence, the middle income group expressed the greatest concern with problems in Fabens. Analyzing the data by ethnicity suggests that Mexican Americans, more so than Anglos, and regardless of income, seemed to be more concerned about unemployment, violence and disorder, and health and welfare services. Both Anglos and Mexican Americans exhibited a similar degree of concern about housing.

It is not surprising that the poor viewed unemployment as more serious a problem than did the rich, or that Mexican Americans expressed greater concern about these social problems than Anglos. Generally, it appears that the closer the issue is to an individual's own everyday experiences, the more likely they were to express a concern. In sum, there were two major stratifying factors regarding social problems: class and ethnicity.

Perceptions About Opportunities in Fabens

Several questions were asked of respondents in order to ascertain their beliefs about upward social mobility, to make money, to actively participate in the political process, and so on.

TABLE 9.2 Opportunities in Fabens by Income Class and Ethnicity (Percentages)

	Plenty of Opportunities	Equal Opportunities to Go to College	Rich and Poor Have Opportunities to Make Money
Income			
Poor	63	30	36
Middle	59	43	37
Rich	90	90	40
% of Sample	**64**	**40**	**37**
Ethnicity			
Mexican-American	59	32	35
Anglo	79	62	37
% of Sample	**64**	**38**	**36**

Source: Notre Dame Research Team.

The first question in Table 9.2 addresses the American ideology: whether a respondent believed there were plenty of opportunities for all to get ahead in America. The rich (90%) expressed the highest degree of agreement, the middle class the lowest. As one affluent respondent stated, "The opportunities are all there, but many don't take them. America is the land of opportunities." Compare this to the female respondent from the middle income group, "Even if there [are] plenty of opportunities in America, there are none in Fabens."

Respondents were also asked if individuals of equal ability also had equal chances of attending college. This particular question received fewer positive responses among the poor and middle income groups; less than a third among the poor agreed, and 43% among the middle income group agreed with the statement. The rich, on the other hand, maintained their high degree of agreement (90%) that there was equality of opportunity to attend college.

A more specific question was asked: Would both the rich and poor have the same opportunities to make the same amount of money if both worked equally hard? All three income groups expressed pessimism about the equality of chances regarding the son of the poor and of the rich to earn an equal amount of money if both worked equally hard. A male respondent from the middle income group responded, "Even though he is not smarter, the son of the rich man will make more money working the same, than the son of the poor man."

In general, the rich held positive views about the opportunity structure in Fabens. Their views coincided to a greater degree than members from the poor and middle income groups on issues pertaining to the American creed. The middle income group and the poor expressed similar views about getting ahead in America. This may be because a large proportion of Mexican Americans are in the middle income group: 67%. The finding also is supported by the results cross tabulated by ethnicity, where on all three questions Mexican Americans expressed a lower degree of optimism than Anglos.

In summary, a majority of all groups acknowledged the existence of a general "opportunity" to get ahead. When asked to become "realists," however, the consensus among all groups is striking. Roughly two thirds of all Fabens residents, regardless of position, recognized a discrepancy in the economic opportunities available to the wealthy in contrast to those available to the less affluent. The recognition of this inequality of economic opportunity, however, did not prevent both rich and Anglo from overlooking equally obvious socioeconomic differences in opportunity for college attendance. This view is all the more surprising given the low college attendance rate among Fabens's youngsters.

Political Opportunity Structure

One aspect of the American creed suggests that being a good citizen is also being a voting citizen. Data displayed in Table 9.3 seem to suggest

TABLE 9.3 Perceptions About Political Opportunities in Fabens

	Voting is Vital	Voting Not the Only Way	People Like Me Have a Say	Poor and Rich Have Equal Influence in Government	Public Officials Care How We Think
	1	2	3	4	5
*Income**					
Poor	84	14	40	24	35
Middle	83	20	52	26	52
Rich	70	40	80	50	90
% of Sample	**82**	**18**	**48**	**27**	**46**
Ethnicity[+]					
Mexican-American	81	10	39	30	39
Anglo	87	33	75	29	67
% of Sample	**83**	**17**	**48**	**30**	**47**

* $n = 118$
[+] $n = 103$
Source: Notre Dame Research Team.

that Fabens residents adhere to such a view. A majority of all three income groups believe voting to be a vital part of being an American citizen.

A second question probed further by focusing on the actual sense of political efficacy among Fabens's citizens—whether they felt and believed they really could have a say in the way government ran things.

Perceptions of political efficacy differed by social class. Thus, though 84% of the poor believed that voting was essential to the political process, and only 14% expressed the belief that there were other ways to have influence, only 24% of the poor believed that their influence in government was equal to that of the rich. There was a clear discrepancy between their right as a citizen, and the reality of their political efficacy. Results for the middle income group were similar to those of the poor, though their sense of political efficacy seemed to be greater. The wealthy, on the other hand, showed a greater degree of consistency: 70% expressed the view that voting was essential, and 40% felt that there were other ways to influence government. Moreover, twice as many rich as poor and middle income respondents believed that the wealthy and the poor had equal influence in government. Somewhat corroborating these findings, less than a third of the poor believed that public officials cared about what people like them felt; by contrast, 90% of the wealthy held the same view. The middle income group expressed views similar to that of the poor.

These results clearly suggest that strong beliefs regarding the importance of voting do not necessarily translate into a sense of political efficacy. The poor seemed to consider voting as vital, but did not believe their votes carried the same weight as their wealthy counterparts.

Controlling for ethnicity, the only striking difference was that obtained in the question about whether people from certain groups (wealthy or poor) have a say in government. About 75% of the Anglos and 39% of Mexican Americans felt they did. In addition, more than two thirds of the Anglos believed that public officials did care about how people like them felt, but only about a third of Mexican Americans expressed a similar belief. In general, then, Mexican Americans held less positive views about their political opportunities than did Anglos.

Concern With Income and Economic Security

The wealthy were more likely than either the poor or middle income groups to be dissatisfied with their income. The middle income groups were the least to be dissatisfied. The wealthy did not perceive themselves as having more economic opportunities than most people, and in general their

TABLE 9.4 Income Concerns in Fabens

	Satisfied with Income	Highly Dissatisfied	Lacking in Income	More Economic Opportunities Than Most People	The Same Economic Opportunities as Most People
Income[*]					
Poor	38	13	67	30	46
Middle	59	9	74	30	59
Rich	50	20	60	40	50
% Sample	**48**	**12**	**69**	**31**	**51**
Ethnicity[+]					
Mexican-American	51	11	73	33	48
Anglo	54		58	29	62
% Sample	**51**	**11**	**70**	**32**	**51**

[*] $n = 119$
[+] $n = 103$
Source: Notre Dame Research Team.

answers tended to indicate less than total satisfaction with their economic opportunities. Data are displayed in Table 9.4.

The middle income group appeared to be most satisfied with their income. Of this group, 74% considered themselves lucky, and only 9% were highly dissatisfied. Whereas 30% of the middle income group believed they had greater economic opportunities than most people, it was not near the 40% among the wealthy who held the same view. On the other hand, 59% of the middle income group felt their economic opportunities to be the same as most people.

Among the poor, 38% said they were satisfied with their income, and 13% were highly satisfied. More poor than wealthy felt lucky with their income, and approximately the same percentage, about half of both groups, believed that they had the same economic opportunities as most people.

Mexican Americans were more likely to hold negative views about their economic chances than Anglos. Forty-eight percent of the Mexican-American respondents and 62% of Anglos believed that they had the same economic opportunities as most people. In addition, 73% of Mexican Americans and 58% of Anglos considered themselves lucky with their income. Thus, even though the majority of Mexican Americans were poor, and less than half believed they had equal opportunities as others, they still held greater feelings of being lucky than Anglos.

Perhaps the most surprising aspect about these responses was the degree of satisfaction expressed by all groups. One would expect, for example, the poor to be dissatisfied with their economic condition, but, on the contrary, only a small proportion was dissatisfied. Even more striking, 76% of the poor and 81% of Mexican Americans claimed to have had the same or more opportunities as other groups. To be sure, the poor exhibited less general satisfaction with their incomes than did the wealthy or middle income groups in Fabens. Thus, the poor and Mexican Americans seemed to be satisfied with their opportunities if not their rewards. Such a discrepancy between the two beliefs suggests that individuals self-blamed for their current statuses. There is a clear lack of understanding of social structure. I examine this in the next section.

Causal Factors of Wealth and Poverty

An important aspect of American folklore is that the poor are poor because they lack personal initiative. As we saw in the previous section, there is the sense that the poor blame themselves for their economic status. We evaluated this folklore by asking respondents a set of questions. Results are presented in Table 9.5.

Interestingly, among the three income groups, the "laziness" factor received the fewest responses for factors explaining the economic condition of the poor. Indeed, structural reasons were given the most responses, and

TABLE 9.5 Reasons for Being Poor

	No Jobs	Poor on Relief: They Are Lazy	Poor Want to Get Ahead	Poor Work as Hard as Others	Poor are Poor Because of Structural Reasons
Income					
Poor	44	14	78	81	56
Middle	43	30	63	70	57
Rich	40	20	90	70	70
% Sample	**44**	**21**	**73**	**76**	**57**
Ethnicity					
Mexican-American	54	13	78	81	59
Anglo	17	50	58	58	40
% Sample	**46**	**21**	**74**	**76**	**56**

Source: Notre Dame Research Team.

the wealthy were more likely to provide such an explanation. Indeed, 70% of the wealthy attributed the plight of the poor to structural reasons, compared to the middle income group (57%), and to the poor (56%).

When the data were stratified by ethnicity, striking differences emerged. Indeed, about 50% of Mexican Americans attributed being on public assistance to a lack of jobs, whereas 17% of Anglos held this belief. Half of the Anglos felt that the poor were on assistance because they were lazy. Moreover, it was Mexican Americans (81%) who felt that the poor work as hard as anyone else. Fifty-eight percent of Anglos expressed this belief.

Wealth and Poverty in Fabens

Issues of wealth and poverty have held the attention of social scientists for many years. During the 1960s the poverty threshold was introduced and immediately established itself as an important social indicator. At that time, the poverty threshold for a family of four was set at less than $3,000. At the same time, economists and other social scientists placed the ability to sustain what is broadly known as the American middle-class way of life at income levels ranging from $5,000 and $10,000 for a family of four. Above $10,000 in income, a family of four is increasingly able to purchase items of comfort and near affluence. I will follow these general economic guidelines in my analysis of the families of Fabens.

Table 9.6 displays the income levels among families in Fabens. In 1960, there were a total of 244 families in our census with incomes under $3,000. This figure represents 40% of all families in Fabens. Another 121 families earned incomes between $3,000 and $4,999. These may be referred to as the near poor, bringing us to a total of 365 families or 61% of all families in Fabens in 1969 with incomes under $5,000 annually.

TABLE 9.6 Household Income in Fabens

Income	Anglo	Mexican American	Black
Poor	25	45	55
Near Poor	9	25	27
Middle	34	25	9
Comfortable	33	3	9
		33	
Sample Size	126	434	11

Note: Poor = less than $3,000; Near Poor = $3,000–$4,999; Middle Income = $5,000–$9,999; Comfortable = $10,000 and over.
Source: Notre Dame Research Team.

At the other end of the income spectrum, 151 families or 35% of all families in Fabens, earned between $5,000 and $9,999 in 1969. In terms of the upper middle income group, there were 55 families, or 9%, of all families in Fabens.

If we focus only on the poor, that is, those with incomes under $3,000 in 1969 and compare this with data from other areas in Texas, the family poverty rate in Fabens is quite high.

Fabens	40%
El Paso County	39%
El Paso City	38%
El Paso outlying area	50%
U.S.	31%
Texas	35%
Corpus Christi	43%
McAllen area	52%
San Antonio outlying area	46%
Uvalde	53%

Two observations can be made from these data. First, Fabens and Texas in general had higher poverty rates than the United States as a whole. Second, it should be kept in mind that the comparison we are making is between Fabens's 1968 reported incomes and the 1966 reported incomes for other areas. Yet another way to examine wealth and poverty in Fabens is by comparing its wealthy to the wealthy in other areas. In this case, those with incomes of $10,000 and over.

Fabens	9%
El Paso County	13%
El Paso City	13%
El Paso outlying area	9%
U.S.	19%
Texas	16%
Corpus Christi	12%
McAllen area	9%
San Antonio outlying area	9%
Uvalde	8%

Again, it would appear that Fabens was below the average for the state of Texas and for the United States as well. Otherwise, the family wealth rate compared favorably with other areas in Texas. It should be noted, however, that areas with which Fabens compared favorably were areas with high proportions of Mexican Americans.

Economic status was not distributed evenly in Fabens. Indeed, Mexican Americans were most likely to be poor, while Anglos affluent. For example, 45% of Mexican-American families in Fabens were under the poverty line compared to 25% of Anglo families. More startling was that 30% of Anglo families earned more than $10,000 annually while only 3% of Mexican-American families earned this much.

For comparative purposes I computed poverty rates for 1960 and 1970. The calculations were computed for Mexican Americans and non-Hispanics in the United States and in Texas. My results are displayed in Table 9.7. These data indicate not only that the poverty rates were greater among Mexican Americans than they were among non-Hispanics, but that the rates were greater in Texas than in the whole of the United States.

Gender also had an effect on economic status in the Fabens community. In fact, 1 out of 5 families indicated that their main source of income was from women rather than men. Most were working women with low-paying jobs. In fact, only 1 woman out of the 124 recorded as heads of household and working earned over $10,000 annually.

Earnings and occupational placement were highly associated. Professionals, proprietors and managers, farm owners, and other white-collar workers were most likely to earn over $10,000. Farm laborers and unskilled, semi-skilled, and service workers were overwhelmingly poor, while professionals were among the middle class and the upper income levels. Three out of four blue collar/service workers earned less than $5,000 annually. White collar workers and skilled workers were more likely to earn more than $5,000 per year.

TABLE 9.7 Poverty Rates Among MA and NH in the USA and in Texas: 1960 and 1970

		MA	NH	Diff
1960	United States	44.3	21.8	22.5
	Texas	63.1	25.9	37.2
1970	United States	26.8	13.5	13.3
	Texas	39.6	14.7	24.9
Diff 1960/1970	United States	–17.5	–8.3	–9.2
	Texas	–23.5	–11.2	–12.3

Source: Notre Dame Research Team.

Low wages for work were not limited to Fabens. Indeed, over half of those travelling to nearby El Paso for work, earned less than $5,000 per year. Given the low educational attainment and limited English speaking abilities, many Fabens residents (Mexican Americans) were forced to accept low wage jobs in Fabens and in El Paso.

Merely bringing more jobs to Fabens would not improve the economic status of many of its citizens. There must also be an effort to increase the wage structure in the community. New jobs would only benefit small retailers who were hurt by the decline of the cotton industry and the ending of the Bracero program. Small retailers would benefit because a larger proportion of Fabens residents would have money to spend. It was the kind of jobs that decision makers hinted at bringing to Fabens that would not alter the income distribution in Fabens.

Poverty forces individuals to leave in search of better employment opportunities elsewhere. The citizens of Fabens were no different. Over half of the poor and near poor were quite mobile, which is not the case for the affluent. Longevity of residing in Fabens did not guarantee moving out of poverty. In fact, both poverty and affluence seemed to be somewhat stable in Fabens. Eighty-two percent of the poor, 80% of the near poor, 77% of the middle income group, but only 67% of the affluent had lived in Fabens 10 or more years. Nevertheless, people preferred to live in Fabens. Between 70 and 80% of persons of all income levels expressed a preference for living in Fabens rather than anyplace else.

Research on the relationship between income group and voluntary association membership indicates a positive association between the propensity to join an association and income group. Data for Fabens supports this finding. Indeed, 84% of the poor were not members of any voluntary association; a third of the middle income group and about half (46%) of the affluent belonged to one or more voluntary associations. To the extent that such organizations provided further channels of communication about local and national affairs, and opportunities to learn something about decision-making at a formal level, the poor were further deprived by their poverty. There are two important points to be made here. First, the poor may not have seen the value in joining such organizations. Second, they may not have felt welcomed by voluntary associations. If voluntary associations are to be viable for the poor, they need to actively recruit members from the poor, and also to ensure that their voices are heard and have access to leadership positions.

Two other areas to which income is related were examined: The possession of common household items, and home ownership. Nearly all Fabens's households had electricity, gas, window and door screens, but ethnic differences begin to emerge regarding running water, television sets, in-house toilets, tubs, and showers. A large proportion of Mexican-American families did not have these items while a large proportion of Anglo families were in possession of such items. For example, about 75% of Mexican-American families did not have telephones, whereas 20% of Anglo families did not have telephones. Again, 40% of Mexican-American families did not have an automobile compared to 14% of Anglo families who did not own an automobile.

In terms of home ownership, a majority of all Fabens owned their homes. The difference occurs in size and quality of these homes. It appears that Anglo homes were larger and in better condition than homes owned by Mexican Americans. Thus, while 7% of Anglo homes had three or fewer rooms, fully 37% of Mexican-American homes were this small or smaller.

Ethnicity, Mobility, and Occupation

About two thirds of Mexican-American household heads reported that some member of their family had left Fabens at some time in the past. This compares with less than 50% of Anglos (see Table 9.8).

Respondents reported that persons leaving were in most cases sons and daughters, or brothers and sisters. It was not possible to gather data on the year in which relatives left Fabens, but it was possible to obtain information on the first two members of the family who had left. These data are reported in Table 9.8, and reveal that a surprisingly large number of both Anglos

TABLE 9.8 Reasons Why First Person Left Fabens

	Anglo	Mexican-American
Better Job	46	64
Job Transfer	10	3
Married	16	16
Health	5	0.7
School/College	3	1
Preferred Urban Environment	2	1
Inherited Land	2	0
Other	6	6
Military Service	8	2
Not Ascertainable	2	6
Total	**61**	**292**

Source: Notre Dame Research Team.

and Mexican Americans left Fabens before 1958. In fact, in 1969, Anglos had a small number of relatives leaving in the previous 5 years compared to the number who left in 1958 or earlier. For Mexican Americans, out migration in 1969 was more balanced with almost as many having left within the previous 5 years as left in 1958 or earlier.

The out migration of Mexican Americans in 1969 or earlier seemed to reflect the declining job opportunities in Fabens. This was supported by the data from an earlier analysis, which shows that the major reasons for leaving Fabens appeared to be better job opportunities elsewhere. Data in Table 9.8 refer to a respondent's perception as to why the first person listed in his/her family left Fabens. Among Anglos, the opportunity to get a better job was frequently mentioned. Among Mexican Americans, job opportunities were the overwhelming reason for having left. The next reason, for both Anglos and Mexican Americans, seemed to have been marriage; and military service, though mentioned, is relatively unimportant.

If job opportunities seem to be an important reason why people left Fabens, it also appears to be a reason for people coming to the community. Indeed, the single most important reason for coming to Fabens appears to be job opportunities in farming or a job transfer. Being near relatives was a reason cited among Mexican Americans, and getting married was a minor reason for both groups.

Of those moving into Fabens, a question was "where people lived before coming to Fabens." We found that Anglos were most likely to have come from El Paso or some other part of Texas. A significant number, however, were from outside the Southwest. Mexican Americans, on the other hand, were most likely to have come from somewhere inside Texas and a larger proportion from Mexico.

Nevertheless, whatever their point of origin, a majority of Fabens residents were highly satisfied with Fabens as a place to live. In fact, a higher percentage of Mexican Americans than Anglos expressed satisfaction of living in Fabens. When asked where they would like to live if not Fabens, Mexican Americans indicated the El Paso area, whereas Anglos suggested an area outside of Texas or even New Mexico.

The occupational characteristics of respondents were examined by ethnicity and not surprisingly Anglos held better jobs than Mexican Americans. Indeed, Anglos were more likely to hold professional and skilled jobs, Mexican Americans were more likely to be employed in unskilled, semiskilled, or farm labor jobs. Only a small percentage of this group held a second job, and a majority of both groups actually worked in Fabens. A significant proportion of Mexican Americans were most likely to be working in the El Paso area and to have held their present job for less than 10 years. In contrast, about one third of Anglos had held their jobs for more than 15 years; this was true for only about 20% of Mexican Americans.

Mexican Americans did not seem to have made any notable progress toward acquiring professional or business occupations while Anglos had. Not only had inequality remained somewhat stable over time, but it was ethnically driven.

In sales and skilled jobs, Mexican Americans made progress. Nevertheless, at the unskilled and semi-skilled labor category, the number of Mexican Americans under age forty was equal to those over age forty. This is disconcerting because, again, it shows a highly stable and stratified labor market.

Summary

A description of Fabens in 1969 shows a community in which Mexican Americans were a numerical majority, but were on the short end of a rigid stratification system. In terms of income, jobs, and education, Mexican Americans did not fare as well as their Anglo counterparts.

Mexican American families tended to be larger than Anglo families, and were crowded in homes that most likely lacked basic amenities such as in-house toilets and baths. Nevertheless, despite their economic status, a vast majority of Mexican Americans were satisfied with Fabens as a place to live.

Appendix

Agriculture

From Clint to the Hudspeth county line, there are 216 separate plots of irrigable bottom land. However, only 151 owners are registered as owning this land—the result of sellouts over past years. The final figure may be reduced even further because as of July, 1969 there were only 105 farmers registered with the U.S. Department of Agriculture (USDA) as actively engaged in farming. One important reason for this is that the number of owners of smaller plots (often under 200 acres) lack the capital to profitably exploit their land and so lease it to larger farmers who have the equipment. As derived from a scattered sample of 30 farmers in the same area, approximately 40% of the active farmers lease one or more pieces of land from others. Ten percent, furthermore, lease cotton allotments from others.

Most farmers were full-time operators. About a third, however, admitted to working off the farm at some other activity within the past 10 years. There were two reasons for working off the farm: the farmer could not make enough from the farm alone, or his outside interest was sufficiently lucrative to be attractive on its own.

Farmers near Clint were smaller than those surrounding the Fabens community and Tornillo, as a result of the encroachment of El Paso. Of the 26 scattered farmers asked to report their own (non-leased) acres, the land holdings shown in Table A.1 were revealed.

The Yellow Rose, pages 115–123

TABLE A.1 Acres Owned (*N* = 26)

Number of Acres	Number of Farmers
1–50	2
51–100	2
101–200	3
201–300	6
301–500	7
501–1,000	4
1,500+	3

Source: Notre Dame Research Team

The average Fabens area farmer's acreage was approximately 300–350 acres in 1969. It is important to note that somewhat less than a quarter of the farms were over 500 acres, and only two in the sample were over 1,000. (The data above, are just a sample and do not comprise the total farms in the Fabens area). The area was thus not one typified by "big spreads." Ethnically, the overwhelming majority of farmers are Anglo. Only 15% of the 216 plots of land in the Fabens area are owned by Mexican Americans.

That 300 to 350 acres appear to be average was not necessarily accidental. It approximates what might be called a "one implement operation" or the size farm which will provide efficient use for one each of the necessary pieces of equipment related to the area's major crops. Less acreage, and a farmer "wastes" part of the cost (initial and upkeep) of his machinery. More acreage and one risks spreading oneself too thin (see Table A.2).

The Fabens farming area lies along bottom land flanking the Rio Grande. The strip of irrigable land is extremely narrow, rarely exceeding 2 or 3 miles in width. The cultivated area is largely of the Harkey-Glendale soil

TABLE A.2 Acres Leased

Number of Acres	Number of Farmers
1–50	3
50–100	1
101–200	1
201–500	4
501–1,000	1
2,500+	1
No leased acres	18

Source: Notre Dame Research Team.

type, nearly level, deep, fine, and medium textured bottom land. Through long use of shallow salty wells prior to and since the creation of the water district, the land has a high salinity. Irrigation and water is thus the major concern of the strictly wetland farmers of the area.

Crops

The lower El Paso Valley is remarkably homogeneous both in crops grown and not grown. By the latter is meant that experimentation visible in the upper valley, for instance, is hardly to be seen in the lower valley. Cotton is the major cash crop and has been for decades. Both short staple and extra-long staple crops are grown in roughly equal quantities. The long staple crop is more expensive to produce, but brings higher prices, and the valley's pima is among the world's best. It should be stressed that many other areas of the world produce similar quality cotton, including Egypt, the Sudan, Peru, and Morocco. Considering that total U.S. production of extra-long staple cotton has averaged around 70,000 bales annually, the Lower El Paso Valley, with roughly 20,000 acres in production of pima, has been supplying over a quarter of the United States' needs.

Cotton allotments amount to roughly 50–60% of cropland in Fabens. Major crops planted on the remainder include alfalfa, milo maize, and barley. Hay and straw are still largely unexploited. Over the last 5 or 6 years, an annual average of 7,000 to 9,000 acres of alfalfa hay has been produced. There is still, however, only one feeder lot of significance in the Fabens area.

Labor and Mechanization

The area's farmers were among the most mechanized in the United States. Since the end of the Bracero program in 1962, farmers have been forced to purchase expensive equipment. This has been one of the major factors behind the consolidation of valley farmers under the guidance of fewer and fewer active farmers with the capital or excess machinery. One typical farmer reports that following the termination of the Bracero program, his annual labor costs fell from $35,000 to $10,000. Nevertheless, the majority of farmers expressed strong resentment over this loss of "cheap labor" which didn't hurt anyone and greatly helped Mexicans. Though bitter at first, farmers today are beginning to change their attitudes toward the "golden" Bracero days. One respondent stated, "If it rained in the old days, you had to keep whatever work force you had and you had to pay them so they wouldn't drift off. Now that we're so highly mechanized, why if it rains, you just shut a machine's motor off."

The average "single implement farm" will maintain from three to five full-time male workers and hire more men "as needed." One farmer says, "I'll hire choppers (weeders) once a season, perhaps in July. I'll just hire 20 men off the street. Whoever comes to my door gets the job. I'll use them for about a week." Hand chopping is still closest and most thorough. Nonetheless, today's farmer limits hand work to once or, at most, twice a season. The remainder of the growing season, mechanical cultivators (both rolling and flame) are used. One farmer estimates that a human chopper can complete an acre in a day at a cost of about $13 (assuming about $1.25 per hour, a figure not always met). One tractor and a rolling cultivator, on the other hand (plus a driver) can do 20 acres for a cost of from $20 to $50, depending upon the age of the tractor and figured depreciation plus maintenance costs. The full-time work force of three to five men is sufficient for most of the year's labor, which includes machine use and irrigation. Some smaller farmers, or those who prefer to get along with less hired help, must hire labor at regular intervals to help with irrigation (which relies largely upon the use of hand-manipulated syphoned tubes).

By and large, half or more of the full-time farm work force is composed of Mexican nationals. They may reside on the farm or across the border in Mexico and commute daily. Though Mexicans are ostensibly "greencarders," information suggests that some, yet I was not able to estimate the numbers, may be illegal. The number of illegal workers hired as choppers is likely much higher than the permanent labor force, as choppers are generally hired "with no questions asked."

One chopping crew interviewed reported earning $1.12 per hour, considerably under the established state minimum wage. "Sometimes we make even less," commented the leader of the crew. "It depends on the wetbacks available. They work for 75¢ an hour and if we want to work, we have to work for the wages they are willing to pay. If we complain, the farmers won't hire us again. What can we do?"

Though resident workers receive free living quarters (usually less comfortable and with fewer facilities than town workers enjoy) their pay is low. Overtime pay is almost unheard of. To boost their incomes, farmers give employees extra, overtime hours, though at their normal hourly rate, so as to "increase their incomes." Experienced foremen rarely earn more than $90–$100 weekly.

Farm Economics

Due to such factors as extremely high irrigation costs, the area's farmers produce cotton at a paper loss, even given minimal labor expenditures. "We must be the most efficient money-losing operation in American business today," comments an officer of the El Paso Valley Cotton Association; and other farmers concur. In 1966, for example, the Upper Rio Grande Trans Pecos and New Mexico region (which includes the Fabens area) showed the highest direct and total costs per pound of all Texas upland cotton producers (200 acres or more). Furthermore, of all Texas regions, this zone showed larger operations (and theoretically more efficient) reporting higher costs per pound than smaller operations (under 50 acres). Farm and Ranch Management (a publication of the Texas A&M AgriLife Extension Service) calls this reversal "somewhat unusual" and illogical. Similarly, research by the Texas A&M experimental station (College Station) pointed out that the same Trans-Pecos, Upper Valley area had the highest production costs among cotton producers in the United States for 1964–1965; and the highest loss per pound, even though the area received the second highest average price per pound of the 15 major cotton producing areas of the United States.

The high costs of cotton production, coupled with the dropping price and demands for cotton are constant items of conversation among cotton farmers in Fabens. Still, constructive action has been pursued. Long-staple consumption in the United States has declined to 127,500 bales in 1967–1968. The latest figures indicate that from 49% in 1967, cotton's percentage of the textile market declined to 43% in 1968. This is not to suggest that cotton will continue to decline in demand. Generally, cotton does not decline in proportion to the increase in demand for synthetics. In 1968, for example, consumption of synthetics increased 20.7% whereas consumption of cotton declined 5%. It is more than likely that cotton demand is bottoming out as certain kinds of cotton-synthetic fabric blends become stable. Similarly, as the population grows, the consumption of cotton may increase even though cotton's share of the textile market may remain stable or actually decline.

It is not likely that U.S. policy concerning foreign long-staple cotton quotas will substantially alter Fabens' farmers' profits in the long run. For a number of years, U.S. imports of long-staple cotton have run at a consistent 82,480 bales annually, or about half the amount consumed by the United States. Farmers complain loudly, yet overlook the fact that so long as U.S. long-staple prices are higher than foreign, textile manufacturers will naturally want to save by purchasing foreign. United States cotton became competitive during the 1968–1969 season when the United States "allowed" domestic cotton prices to fall so as to make local growers more competitive. The result was lower profit for the farmer even though, as in this instance, only 24,500 bales of foreign long-staple entered the country, the lowest quota in a decade (U.S. Bureau of Customs, Records, 1969).

Of 28 farmers responding to a question about the future of cotton, only 2–7%, indicated firm faith in its continued "success." Eighteen percent felt that the future of cotton was uncertain, that it faced many problems. Almost 70% were pessimistic, feeling that cotton's future was weak.

In 1969, farmers have given much discussion to diversification. Indeed, over half the sampled farmers said they were presently considering some kind of diversification. The emotional attachment to cotton is indicated by the inordinate conversation over "vertical" rather than "horizontal" diversification. Vertical refers to other aspects of cotton treatment, particularly milling. Horizontal refers to farming other types of crops. In either case, little has resulted from these discussions, though the local cotton association has acquired control over a local fertilizer firm.

Among the sample of farmers asked to evaluate produce production in the valley, only 7% felt that it had been successful. Fifty-four percent felt that the success of produce was variable and dependent upon many factors such as marketing, soil, and so forth. Twenty-seven percent felt produce had been successful in the valley. The remaining 12% "did not know" (i.e., had not bothered to inform themselves or had not thought seriously about the problem). Twenty-three of 29 farmers sampled (almost 80%) have never planted produce. Of those who have, over half report planting less than 15 acres at any one time. Prior to 1965 no lettuce acreage was recorded in the El Paso County Water District #1. In 1965 only 50 acres were recorded, with 132 acres in 1966. In 1968, 897 acres of lettuce were reported, or slightly over 1% of the roughly 71,000 total cultivated acres in the valley. Onions have averaged only 100 to 200 acres annually in the entire valley, with 232 planted in 1968. Tomatoes have averaged approximately 200 acres annually, with only 50 being recorded in 1968. Sorghum has tripled in 5 years to 1,746.

Thus, vegetable production can hardly be called "experimental" as yet. Vegetables ostensibly represent a great potential profit. In 1968, for example, the Bureau of Reclamation evaluated El Paso County's onion crop at $730 per acre, and lettuce at $1,133.

The valley's reluctance to significantly diversify is due largely to a "self-fulfilling prophesy." That is, farmers have had little success with vegetables because they are afraid to enter serious production; their limited efforts are not sufficient to overcome the risks involved. So they do in fact lose money on their minimal plantings which further confirms to them their belief that diversification won't work.

"You can make it with lettuce if you hit two years out of five," say area farmers, and this amazing affirmation of inefficiency is echoed by the county conservation district newsletter. Certainly, few industries of any kind could exist with such a profit time-table. By and large, even this estimate is based on the fact that through purely fortuitous circumstances, other, well-established lettuce producing areas of the United States either lose a crop 2 years out of 5, or that 2 years out of 5 in the valley (and other loose, sporadic vegetable producing areas) due to local climatic phenomena, produce a harvestable crop somewhat in advance of, or behind, the major producers, and thus fill a void which in other years might not exist.

Thus, vegetable production is closely tied to "luck" in valley farmers' minds, scarcely a condition favoring serious, and thus more success-prone diversification attempts.

The developing pecan production in the valley is yet another indication of more or less non-serious attempts at agricultural diversification. Most view such operations as Stahman's in New Mexico with envy and/or admiration.

Such success stories have spurred scores of Valley farmers into planting seedlings. Few have investigated and projected the potential pecan market into the late nineteen-seventies when their trees and the trees of perhaps hundreds of more similarly eager local planters will have reached maturity. In 1968, the Conservation District reports that the county's 315 acres of producing pecans were worth $310 an acre—far less than onions or lettuce for the same year.

As a group, valley farmers have done little to increase the area's economic base. The El Paso Valley Cotton Association was founded originally as the local representative of cotton producers within a regional and a national interest group. Four cotton organizations are represented in the valley: the El Paso Valley Cotton Association, the Texas Association of Cotton Producer Organizations (TACPRO), the Five States Cotton Growers, and the National Cotton Council. Local farmers have served all four as officers and as representatives. Only the El Paso Valley Cotton Association has taken an active step towards broadening the Fabens economic base. Several years ago the Cotton Association sponsored the establishment of the El Paso Valley Development Corporation, a body which would investigate and implement agricultural diversification within the valley. Its expressed goals were to implement vertical diversification within cotton, and foment interests in other activities such as vegetables, pecans, feed grain storage, and livestock feeding. Indeed, not long after its founding, the corporation purchased South West Fertilizer. Actually, the purchase makes little or no difference to individual farm profits. As one farmer put it, "more than anything, the purchase of South West Fertilizer gives us one more common bond—something to hold us farmers together. Dues alone (to the cotton association) can't bind people." Of 27 farmers responding to questions of their membership, 22, or approximately 80%, claimed to be members of the El Paso Valley Cotton Association. Only 38% of the farmers interviewed were members of any other agricultural association or associations. Indeed, of those claiming membership in the El Paso Cotton Association, 64% admitted to being only "passive" members.

"Passivity" being a reflection of the fact that the valley farmer is still making a living (albeit not a spectacular one characterizes the valley farmer). While farmers are not necessarily critical about either the extension service or the Texas A&M experimental station, few take an active part in making sure that such services fully meet local needs. As one farmer noted of a large USDA arranged meeting in El Paso last year: "80 experts, agents, and professors were there, and only eight dirt farmers. They just can't get themselves organized or moving." Similarly, while a number of farmers complained that the A&M experimental station is steadfastly working with cotton improvement despite local interest in and needs for specific advice and developments in vegetable and other diversified production, few if any have done more than complain. Most farmers, in fact, are aware of the A&M research, but few are sure of what specifically the group is doing beyond "ways to improve cotton."

Overall, there appears to be no general opinion as to what the valley "really" needs. It is instructive to view responses from farmers to the question of what the valley needs most (see Table A.3). The variety of these

TABLE A.3 What the Valley Needs Most

What the Valley Needs Most	Farmers
Better irrigation system	5
Crop diversification	5
Industrialization	5
Better prices and market	4
Establishment of a co-op	2
No improvement is possible	1
Don't know	2

Source: Notre Dame Research Team

responses indicates a lack of consensus and by implication lack of adequate discussion among farmers and related agri-business regarding the issues facing the industry.

References

Ahearn, D. J. (1945). The wages of farm and factory laborers, 1914–1944. New York, NY: Columbia University Press.

Alston, L. J. (1983). Foreclosures in the United States during the interwar period. *Journal of Economic History, 43*(4), 885–903.

Alvarez, R. (1973). The psycho-historical and socioeconomic development of the Chicano community in the United States. *Social Science Quarterly, 53*(4), 920–942.

Averitt, R. (1968). *The dual economy.* New York, NY: W. W. Norton.

Baran, P., & Sweezy, P. (1966). *Monopoly capital: An essay on the American economic social order.* New York, NY: Monthly Review Press.

Barrera, M. (1981). *Race and class in the Southwest: A theory of racial inequality.* South Bend, IN: University of Notre Dame Press.

Billington, R. A. (1974). *Western expansion: A history of the American frontier.* New York, NY: Macmillan.

Bierstedt, R. (1963). *The social order: An introduction to sociology.* New York, NY: Macmillan.

Blalock, H. H. (1967). *Toward a theory of minority group relations.* New York, NY: Wiley.

Blank, R. M., Dabady, M., & Citra, C. F. (Eds.). (2004). *Measuring racial discrimination.* Washington, DC: National Academies Press.

Browning, H. L., & McLemore, D. S. (1964). *A statistical profile of the Spanish-surname population of Texas.* Austin: University of Texas Press.

Camarilo, A. (1979). *Chicanos in a changing society: From Mexican pueblos to American barrios in Santa Barbara and Southern California, 1848–1930.* Cambridge, MA: Harvard University Press.

The Yellow Rose, pages 125–128

Coleman, J. S. (1962). The adolescent society: The social life of the teenager and its impact on education. New York, NY: The Free Press.

Dickens, W., & Lang, K. (1993). Labor market segmentation theory: Reconsidering the evidence. In W. Darity Jr. (Ed.), Labor economics: Problems in analyzing labor markets (pp. 141–180). New York, NY: Springer.

Doeringer, P., & Piore, M. (1972). Internal labor markets and manpower analysis. Lexington, MA: D. C. Heath.

Garcia, M. T. (1981). *Desert immigrants: The Mexicans of El Paso, 1880–1920.* New Haven, CT: Yale University Press.

González, N. (1967). *The Spanish Americans of New Mexico: A heritage of pride.* Albuquerque, NM: University of New Mexico Press.

Harrison, B., & Sum, A. (1979). The theory of "dual" or segmented labor markets. *Journal of Economic Issues, 13*(3), 687–706.

Hodges, H. M. (1964). *Social stratification: Class in America.* Cambridge, MA: Schenkham.

Jamieson, S. M. (1945). Labor unionism in American agriculture (Bulletin of the U.S. Bureau of Labor Statistics, No. 836). Washington, DC: U.S. Government Printing Office.

Johnston, L., & Williamson, S. H. (2019). *What was the U.S. GDP then?* Retrieved from the Measuring Worth website: http://www.measuringworth.org/usgdp/

Lieberson, S. (1961). A societal theory of race and ethnic relations. *American Sociological Review, 26,* 902–910.

Lenski, G. (1966). *Power and privilege: A theory of social stratification.* New York, NY: McGraw-Hill.

Mannheim, K. (1936). Ideology and utopia. London, England: Routledge.

Marx, K. (1887/1995). *Das kapital, Volume 1.* New York, NY: Penquin Classics.

McWilliams, C. (1990). *North from Mexico: The Spanish-speaking people of the United States.* Westport, CT: Praeger. (Originally published in 1948)

Meier, M. S., & Rivera, F. (1972). The Chicanos: A history of Mexican Americans. New York, NY: Hill and Wang.

Mills, W. W. (1962). *Forty years at El Paso.* El Paso, TX: Carl Hertzog.

Montejano, D. (1992). *Anglos and Mexicans in the making of Texas, 1836–1986.* Austin, TX: University of Texas Press.

Montgomery, D. (1987). The fall of the house of labor: The workplace, the state, and American labor activism. Cambridge, England: Cambridge University Press.

Moore, J. W. (1970). Colonialism: The case of the Mexican Americans. *Social Problems,* 17: 463–472.

Moore, J. W., & Cuellar, A. (1970). *Mexican Americans.* Englewood Cliffs, NJ: Prentice Hall.

North, D. C. (1966). *The economic growth of the United States*: 1790–1860. New York, NY: Norton.

Officer, L. H., & Williamson, S. H. (2019a). *The Annual Consumer Price Index for the United States, 1774–Present.* Retrieved from the MeasuringWorth website: http://www.measuringworth.com/uscpi/

Officer, L. H., & Williamson, S. H. (2019b). *Annual Wages in the United States, 1774–Present.* Retrieved from the Measuring Worth website: http://www.measuringworth.com/datasets/uswage/

Ogbu, J. (1978). *Minority education and caste: The American system in cross cultural perspective.* New York, NY: Academic Press.

Olsen, M. E. (1970). Power perspectives in stratification and race relations. In M. E. Olsen (ed.), *Power in Societies.* New York, NY: Macmillan.

Overton, M. (1996). *Agricultural revolution in England: The transformation of the Agrarian economy, 1500–1850.* Cambridge, MA: Cambridge University Press.

Perkins, Van Lee. (1969). Crisis in agriculture: The agricultural adjustment administration and the new deal, 1933. Berkeley, CA: University of California Press.

Piore, M. (1972). *Notes for theory of labor market stratification* (Working Paper No. 95, Department of Economics). Cambridge, MA: MIT.

Portes, A., & Rumbaut, R. G. (2001). Legacies: The story of the immigrant second generation. Berkeley, CA: University of California Press.

Ransford, H. E. (1977). Race and class in American society: Black, Chicano, Anglo. Cambridge, MA: Schenkman.

Reich, M., Gordon, D. M., & Edwards, R. C. (1973). Dual labor markets: A theory of labor market segmentation. *American Economic Review, 63*(2), 359–365.

Renshaw, P. (1967). *The wobblies.* Garden City, NY: Doubleday.

Reschenthaler, P. (1968). Postwar readjustment in El Paso, 1945–1950. El Paso, TX: Texas Western University.

Rosenthal, R., & Jacobson, L. (1968). *Pygmalion in the classroom.* New York, NY: Holt, Rinehart, and Winston.

Ruggles, S., Genadek, K., Goeken, R., Grover, J., & Sobek, M. (2015). Integrated public use microdata series: Version 6.0 [Machine-readable database]. Minneapolis: University of Minnesota.

Ruggles, S., Genadek, K., Goeken, R., Grover, J., & Sobek, M. (2017). Integrated public use microdata series: Version 7.0 [dataset]. Minneapolis: University of Minnesota.

Sonnichsen, C. L. (1968). *Pass of the north.* El Paso, TX: Texas Western Press.

Spring, J. (1976). *The sorting machine: National educational policy since 1945.* New York, NY: McKay.

Thompson, E. P. (1963). The making of the English working class. New York, NY: Alfred A. Knopf.

Turner, M. (1984). Enclosures in Britain, 1750–1830. In L. A. Clarkson (Ed.), *The Industrial Revolution: A Compendium* (pp. 211–295). London, England: Palgrave.

United States. (1951). *Migratory labor in American agriculture: Report of the president's commission on migratory labor.* Washington, DC: GPO.

Verdugo, R. R. (1986). Educational stratification and Hispanics. In M. A. Olivas (Ed.), *Latino College Students.* New York, NY: Teachers College Press.

White, O. (1924). *Out of the Desert.* El Paso, TX: McMath.

Wilson, W. J. (1973). Racism, power, and privilege: Race relations in theoretical and socio-historical perspectives. New York, NY: Macmillan.

Young, J. R. (2002). Conversations with General Grant. Baltimore, MD: The Johns Hopkins University Press.

Printed and bound by CPI Group (UK) Ltd, Croydon, CR0 4YY

15/09/2026

14962335-0007